A novel by...

BEATRICE BRADSHAW

Book #2 in the Scottish Rugby Rebels series

Falling in love wasn't part of the game plan...

FINN

Rugby's the only thing holding me together. But one huge scandal, and I'm about to lose it all. The press are circling. The sponsors want me gone. My only shot? Fake a relationship with Theodora MacMickin and convince the world I've changed. Trouble is, I'm starting to want what I'm only meant to sell.

THEO

After my ex wrecked my career, I rebuilt my life and landed my dream job. Now the agency's future rests on me fixing Finn Lennox's mess. Make the media believe he's in love, keep him out of trouble, keep my distance.
But fake-dating Scottish rugby's biggest bad boy isn't simple – especially when it starts to feel more and more real…

Sign up for Beatrice's newsletter here!

Content Note

Rucked Up Ruse is written in British English ('recognise' instead of 'recognize'). It also includes a hint of a Scottish accent here and there (see glossary at the end).

Please be aware: this book contains several explicit/smutty open-door sex scenes and a good amount of profanity. Reader discretion is advised.

It also touches on topics that could be triggering for some readers, including anxiety and panic attacks, gaslighting, being temporarily unhoused, substance abuse and addiction, incarceration, the death of an estranged parent, parental neglect and abuse, as well as depression. Most of it is in the backstory, but it's best to be prepared.

Take care of yourself. <3

*To all the wee souls whose parents failed them:
it was not your fault.*

Prologue

Finn

A m I dead?

The floor's cold. Which wouldn't be a problem if I weren't face down on it, naked and confused. My cheek's stuck to the stone tiles, something sticky matted in my hair. Could be champagne, could be lube. My bet's on both.

I should be laughing. But there's this quiet dread under my ribs, like I've opened my eyes underwater and can't remember how to swim.

I lift my hungover head and immediately regret it. Someone groans behind me. Female, definitely. There's a leg draped over mine. Smooth, tanned, and freshly waxed. Painted toes with French tips. But nothing clicks. I stare, waiting for memory to kick in and say, *Aye, mate, you're grand. That's Chloe or Frankie you met at the bar…*

Nothing.

This is what I get for thinking I could outrun the shitshow

that is my life. For thinking Finn Lennox could forget who he is for a week and go on the epic mother of all benders.

Another groan, a different voice this time.

Two women? Christ, what happened last night?

I push myself upright, slow and careful, because the wrong move might trigger a nuclear event inside my throbbing head. Dull, thick waves that are synced to my heartbeat. There's a fur throw…or something like it…dangled over the end of the bed. I stagger over, wrap it around me as if I were some cursed Viking chief, and survey the battlefield.

Crumpled silk sheets and crystal glasses with bits of ash floating in the bottom. A teddy on the windowsill, half-soaked and strangled in a lace bra. Knickers on the curtain rod and a single ski boot in the fireplace. Next thing I notice are olives smashed into the sheepskin rug.

Minging.

Even through the hangover haze, I clock the torn foils glinting on the couch. Evidence I didn't gamble with safety. I bagged up. Thank fuck.

There's got to be a phone somewhere. Not mine, that's still in Scotland. But someone's. I need to know what time it is. What damned *day*.

I stumble toward a coffee table with half-eaten chocolate strawberries, a tequila bottle, a clutch bag the size of a dinner roll, and a few pills scattered between them. I don't do pills, don't touch that stuff. Never needed more than rugby, a drink, and a bit of sex to take the edge off. Gave up booze a year ago. Not one drop, at least until…

Aye, I got steamin' from Christmas all the way to Hogmanay to numb the pain and the grief of losing a father I never even knew.

I look inside the clutch: tampons, gum, lipstick, and an iPhone. I hit the screen.

1st January. 10:42 am.

New year, new rock bottom.

The lock screen is a golden retriever in a Santa hat. Cute dog that looks like he's got more emotional stability than me. But, to be honest, that's not hard.

The upper corner of the screen says St. Moritz, CH. Switzerland. That checks out, sort of. I look back at the fireplace. Must be a ski chalet. A bolt hits my stomach with memory fragments. Kit. That posh git brought me to the Alps for the holidays, right after…

You'd think I'd feel something by now. Shame, maybe. Relief. But it's just static. I blink hard, hoping this scene will rearrange itself into something familiar. I get only flashes. A hot tub. Fireworks. Me screaming *'I will never die!'* off the balcony like the hopeless eejit I am.

I sit on the edge of the bed. The throw glides off my shoulders. Slowly, I lower my head.

There's glitter on my boaby.

Goddammit, Finn.

And inside me there's a muted scream. I won't let it out. If I let it out, I won't stop.

The brunette on the floor giggles in her sleep. I watch her for a second, then the blonde one on the bed. They both look fine, pleased, and blissed out. Like they had a good night and no regrets.

Good. That's what matters.

I don't remember everything, but I do remember laughing. Mutual fun for all parties involved, that's my motto. Even when I'm off my rocker, I'm respectful.

I'd love to say, 'My maw raised me right.' But she didn't raise me. She barely put up with me before she threw me out.

The one on the bed has kicked her duvet off. I get up, shuffle closer, and bend down to tuck it back over her legs. The brunette on the floor's got nothing. I drape the fur throw over her, hoping that's enough. I want them warm and safe.

Briefly, I think about lifting her onto the bed, but I don't want to wake her, and I'm probably too wobbly anyway. Then

I pace toward the enormous windows, part the curtain with one shaking hand, and pull it aside.

The view's too sharp and bright. My eyes blur, then refocus. Whitewashed Alps, chalets – no, lodges? cabins? – stacked like biscuits. Swiss flags flap everywhere, red with that prim white cross. It's pretty, in a way that almost pisses me off. The Highlands are rougher and wetter. Gloomier and grittier, but also more honest.

I should miss home.

But 'home' is a weird word. Doesn't sit right in my mouth. Not sure what it means, or exactly what I'm meant to miss. Certainly not the former mining sinkhole that's Duncraig where I had to move when I signed the contract as a flanker last March. Maybe my team. The Stirling Rebels aren't half bad.

Below, on the snowy street, someone's got a camera pointed at the hotel entrance. A long lens. Paparazzi. Or I'm paranoid. I flinch away from the window. I need to leave. Find Kit and deck him. Or perhaps thank him. Depends on what happened here.

A knock at the door. The blonde woman lets out a little sigh.

Another knock.

Jesus. Pull it together.

I shuffle to the door, and inch it open. Kit Lascelles-Finch, right on cue, wearing sunglasses indoors like a wanker. God knows what he's hiding beneath them. He's always been up to something.

We met at the academy in our late teens. A privately educated toff and a lad from the schemes, two players who hated authority more than each other. We mostly lost touch after he flamed out of the sport. I went to two of his birthday parties. After that, just the odd social media sighting.

So why the hell did I call *him* on Christmas Eve?

Rucked Up Ruse

Because I didn't know who else to phone, and I was fucking wrecked and needed out.

'Finlay Lennox! You're alive,' he declares. 'But barely, by the looks of it.'

My full name in his Etonian lilt makes me want to puke, but that's probably the tequila. 'Where the fuck were you, man?'

'Left shortly before three.' A sleazy grin spreads over his face. 'You said you wanted both sisters to yourself.'

A surge of nausea creeps up my throat. '*Sisters*?'

'Technically stepsisters, so relax. No blood, just old money.' He lifts a shoulder, still grinning. 'And who am I to stand in the way of you shagging nobility? Something about "bridging the class divide" and proving "rugby players aren't just brawn".' His grin kicks up another notch. 'Well done, you.'

'Jesus, Kit. What the hell?' But I don't ask for details. I don't want them.

'You were in quite a state.' Another lazy shoulder roll. 'We all self-destruct in our own way. Yours happens to be scandalous shagging. Could be worse. Breakfast or a round of skiing?'

I let out a pained groan. 'You wish.'

'I see. Come to Badrutt's when you're ready to face the world again.'

'Don't think so, mate.' I shut the door and lean against it, heart tripping over itself.

Finn Lennox. Professional rugby player. Casual power shagger. Regular fuckup.

I catch sight of myself in the mirror. Just a glimpse. Bile rises when the glass throws my da's eyes straight back at me. The same light shade of blue, the same look and the face... All of it. I don't want his fucking eyes. I don't want anything from him. I wish I could delete him from my consciousness, the way he did with me. Until it was too late to fix things.

The panic claws up so fast I have to turn away. It starts in my spine. My throat clamps shut. Vision tunnels. I brace myself on the doorframe. Try to breathe, but the air won't go in. My chest seizes, heartbeat's gone rabid.

C'mon. Breathe. In. Out. In and out.

I picture the pitch. The sound of studs on turf. A line-out call. Anything but this.

Gradually, the iron band around my torso loosens.

There's a hollow in my chest where something else should be. And perhaps I went on this bender to fill it. Or maybe I did it hoping someone would notice. No fucking clue.

I know only one thing for sure. Whatever happened here the past few days, it's gonna cost me.

Chapter 1

Theo

One matcha latte and one oat milk cappuccino. Tick. Invoices filed, Charlie's diary clear until three. Double-tick. Social postings scheduled. Triple tick. If organisation were an Olympic sport, I'd be draped in gold, singing *Flower of Scotland* at the top of my lungs.

Last night, I alphabetised my spice rack – from cinnamon to turmeric. What can I say? I like to begin the new year with outer order and inner peace.

Even if both never last beyond January.

Two days in, Edinburgh is a slushy grey mess of broken resolutions and discarded Christmas trees. Scottish January wind rattles the windows of this former warehouse turned co-working space. Inside Elite Edge Sports Management's office, however, calm prevails. Mostly because I enforce it with the efficiency of a benevolent, caffeinated despot. That's my job as assistant, after all, and I take that seriously.

Also, everybody else in the world is still at home, nursing their monumental Hogmanay hangovers.

I don't drink. Am I a workaholic?

Possibly, possibly.

But I *do* have something to prove. Being kicked out of a

global agency like Nectar London wreaks havoc on anyone's confidence. Yeah, I tanked my first proper job, and it wasn't even my fault. Unless you count gullibility.

The radiator in my tiny office hisses and clanks. The converted warehouse aesthetic might seem sexy on our website, but the heating system belongs in a museum.

'Theo?' My boss Charlotte Harrington's voice cuts through the glass wall. 'Got a minute?'

I grab my notepad and battered, glittery travel mug, and make my way into her office next door. My reflection bounces back at me in the partition. Wonky fringe, toner streak on my cherry-print blouse, and a high ponytail that resembles that of a wee Shetland horse at a rave.

'Professional competence at its finest,' I deadpan and smooth back the escaped strands.

She's hunched over her laptop, hair twisted into that messy bun she turns into a statement. Wish I could pull that off.

'Did you reschedule the MacInnes interview?'

'Moved it to Thursday, ten sharp. He'll be charming, guaranteed.'

Andy MacInnes, the cyclist, is one of our so-called heritage clients, like Brodie MacRae. They came with the list when Charlie acquired Henderson's sports management last year.

She gives me a wry smile. 'You make it look so easy.'

'It's who I am. Anything else?'

She shakes her head. 'No. But honestly, you're the glue that holds this whole thing together.'

'That's on my CV under special skills.'

Yep. The unshakeable Theodora MacMickin, purveyor of order, slayer of chaos, and secret hoarder of sparkly mugs and matcha. If only I could sort my anxieties as easily as my spices.

Just as I'm about to leave, a ping from her phone makes me turn around. She snatches it up, pink creeping over her face like a sunrise over the Firth of Forth. That tell-tale flush you get when you're trying not to look bashful.

And I should know – chronic blushing is the bane of my existence. Honestly, it's debilitating.

'Everything alright there, boss?' I lift the corner of my mouth.

She startles, tucking her phone away. 'Yeah…erm…just Brodie.'

I'm physically incapable of resisting the jab. 'Sexting at work is it now?'

Charlie's my boss. But she's also become a close friend. She's twenty-six, only one year older than me, and I admire her. That woman has balls bigger than most of the oh-so-tough athletes she represents.

She glows, and my face does that thing where it won't stop smiling. I'm truly pleased to see her so happy. She deserves someone who worships the ground she walks on. Someone who isn't a manipulative, gaslighting, lying tosser. Unlike her father and her ex-fiancé, Brodie hadn't stomped all over her heart and left it looking like roadkill.

The memory of my own betrayal still sits low in my gut and tastes awful, even a year on. Like licking a penny. Love came, conquered, destroyed me, and sent me crawling back to Scotland with shattered dreams.

'Brodie's picking me up later.' Charlie fiddles with the pen in her hand.

'Ooh, another date night. You two are disgusting. Cute, but gross.'

She chucks a crumpled paper ball at me and misses by a mile. 'And you're terrible,' she says, but her grin is genuine.

'Maybe. But he's clearly very good for you.'

Too bad that no one had ever been that good for me. The thought sparks and dissolves. No time for self-pity.

'He is,' she says with a dreamy look in her eyes. 'He really is.'

They're moving in together, only a few months into their relationship. Makes complete sense for them. I've never seen anyone so head-over-heels in love as Brodie MacRae and Charlotte Harrington.

'Now, if you'll excuse me, I have a reputation for ruthless efficiency to uphold.' I turn to go, smoothing down my skirt. The world might be a chaotic mess, but my life, at least, remains impeccably arranged.

'Thanks, Theo.'

Back in my own tiny office, the faint drone of the computer sounds strangely oppressive. Ruthless efficiency – that's the fortress I've cultivated, brick by painstaking brick. Made of competence, designed to keep the world at bay.

London taught me the dangers of vulnerability the hard way. Gil had promised me the world, then nuked it and handed me the ashes. By the time I realised the extent of his fucked-up game, it was too late.

No. I won't let him haunt me, not even on a dreary Thursday in January. I have work to do, an empire to build, and reputations to polish. And if Charlie's happy, and I had a hand in that, good. That's enough. Love might be a superpower, as I'd told her the other day, but it's also a volatile one. Best to admire it from a safe distance, armed with a well-organised to-do list.

Men. Who needs them? They're a bonus, not a necessity.

I finally have a thriving career, a curated spice rack, and a cute cat who just about tolerates my existence. What more could a woman in her mid-twenties want?

'What the fucking FUCK?!'

My mug tips, spilling matcha across the desk. Instinct kicks in before thought, and my body's moving. I burst into Charlie's office without knocking.

'What on earth happened?' I sound calm while emerging

panic flurries inside. It could be anything – her father, her ex, a full-on apocalypse…

Her gaze is glued to her laptop. 'Check this out. Unbelievable.'

She angles the screen my way. The email subject line reads:

REQUEST FOR COMMENT – FINN LENNOX SCANDAL

My stomach plummets. I scan the text, and words jump out like neon signs: tabloid…publishing tomorrow…photos attached…Swiss resort…New Year's Eve…Lord Dalcrieff's fiancée and her stepsister…explicit content…

I click the attachment.

Oh.

Oh *damn*.

Two women, one blonde and one brunette, both on their knees. Finn Lennox, pink-haired flanker extraordinaire and our newest acquisition, sitting between them on a couch. The picture is grainy but clear enough.

'Bloody rugby players,' I mutter under my breath. 'Someone's got to stop these man-babies making a mess, wrecking their careers, and giving their agency grief.'

'Switzerland.' She pushes away from her desk. *'That's* where he disappeared over the holidays. That's why he didn't answer any of my calls, texts, or emails.'

She paces, her heels stabbing the floor. I keep scrolling through the images, each more incriminating than the last. But… he's got an impressive piece of kit, I have to give him that.

Highly inappropriate. Moving on.

'When did you last speak to him?' I ask quickly to steer my thoughts in any other direction.

'Christmas Eve. His text said he needed some space after a family bereavement. Then he went AWOL.'

'Right.' I reset my posture and square up. 'First, we need to verify these photos are real.'

'They are. Look at his hair and tattoos. God, the headline. They're calling it "The Double Snow Job".'

A hysterical laugh bubbles up my throat. I swallow it down in the last second. 'Bad, but catchy.'

'This could torch everything.' She stops pacing and braces herself against her desk. 'The car dealership contract I've been negotiating. The Rebels' current sponsorships. His reputation. Their reputation. Our reputation. Hell, this entire agency! Lord Dalcrieff is a sitting Tory MP, and he's not going to be amused.'

My brain clicks into crisis mode. This is what I do, I fix things and make order from chaos. But even I feel cold sweat breaking out across my shoulder blades.

'We need to contact Finn.' I say. 'Get his side of the story. Did he know about the Tory MP connection? Did he know they were sisters – stepsisters, whatever? Was he…drugged? We need information. Where is he?'

'How the fuck should I know? Jesus! Why didn't I go into accounting or banking or zoo keeping?'

I keep my tone level. 'Has he returned to Scotland, do you know?'

She checks her phone. 'According to Brodie, he's missed the conditioning sessions, but is expected back for full intensity training tomorrow.'

'Good. That's good.' I'm already scribbling. 'We have to prepare a statement. Contrite but not admitting liability.'

'They've got photos of him getting enthusiastically serviced by two women, one of whom happens to be engaged to a fucking Tory MP! How much more liable does it get?'

I pause my pen mid-word. 'Yeah. The politics angle complicates things.'

'You think?' Her laugh is bitter. 'Elite Edge is eight months old. Eight months. And I signed him just before Christmas, fully aware of his volatility. What got into me? Am I clinically insane?'

The guilt in her voice makes my chest tighten. 'This isn't your fault, Charlie.'

'Isn't it? I should have known better. But... I like the guy.'

'He's brilliant on the pitch,' I say quietly. 'Always has time for the fans, grins like a wee boy when he scores as if he can't believe his luck. No off switch. The fans love him. So does the team.'

'We'll see how long that's going to last.' She sinks into her chair. 'And management could drop him, although that's unlikely mid-season.'

I drum my pen against the paper. 'We have to get ahead of this and control the narrative.'

'How? What are we gonna say – they just used his dick as a microphone for an impromptu naked karaoke session?'

I snort-laugh. 'Aye, but... They're also private and taken without consent. We can spin this as an invasion of privacy, you know? Like Hasselhoff and the cheeseburger?' My stomach twists with anxiety, but I push through it. 'We need Finn here.'

Charlie reaches for her phone. 'I'll try Scottie. They're living together and are quite pally.'

'And I'll draw up three potential statements.' I head for the door, then pause. 'Charlie?'

'What?'

'We'll fix this.' I'm not one hundred per cent convinced, but she needs to hear it.

'Will we?' Her eyes meet mine, vulnerable in a way I rarely see. 'Because this feels like the beginning of the end.'

Her words drop into me, right where doubt and fear live. Elite Edge isn't just a job for me. It's redemption and a second chance after the agency job in London crushed me. If we go down because of Finn Lennox's childish inability to keep his tadger in his trousers, I'm not sure what I'll do.

This is why I keep my life so ordered. Once you let chaos in, it spreads like wildfire, consuming everything in its path.

'Well then.' She exhales and straightens her shoulders. The strategist is back. 'Plan B. We contain the leak. We contact the tabloid and offer them an exclusive. We'll send out a carefully worded statement, a photo of Finn looking appropriately remorseful. We minimise the damage and protect the team. We salvage what we can.'

Her fingers rest lightly on the keyboard, all steady now. The Charlie I know, love, and respect is emerging from the rubble of initial shock. The Charlie who gave everyone the manicured middle finger and started her own sports management agency. This is more like it. Action, not panic. Control, not chaos.

'I'll get the coffee, boss. Industrial-strength.' I'm already calculating how many espresso shots we'll need to survive the next twenty-four hours. 'Then I'll outline the statements. And start calling the sponsors.'

'What would I do without you, Theo?'

'Commit homicide, probably. Let's save Finn's career first. Then you can butcher him at your leisure.' I offer her a tight smile. 'We'll get through this. Elite Edge is going to be huge, Charlie. Mark my words. We'll be the biggest sports agency in Scotland.'

I mean it. I'm going to bust my butt to make that happen. Men might come and go – but our friendship, our shared ambition, that's the real love story. The one I'm determined to see through to its happily ever after.

Chapter 2

Finn

I'm sitting in one of Charlie Harrington's chairs, legs sprawled in a way that says I don't give a fuck.

Except I do. Wouldn't be here if I didn't.

My right knee bounces as if it's got its own heartbeat. I'm early, she's late. Maybe grabbing a coffee to buy herself two more minutes of not having to deal with me. Mac, one of the few people on Charlie's team, let me in and said she'd be right back.

I check my phone. 11:23.

By now, they'll be lowering him into the ground. I wonder if anyone's crying, if my maw is there. I highly doubt it, she hated my father. And he didn't have friends as far as I know, except the mates he made in prison. My guess is it's one or two surviving drug pals and a minister who's never met him. Something's wedged between my ribs, growing sharper by the minute.

I'm not at my father's funeral because I'd rather be anywhere else. Even here, about to be skinned alive by my new agent.

I force the knot lower.

The door opens, and Charlie breezes in, tablet tucked

under her arm. No shouting or stomping. Only a calm, collected agent in her crisp white shirt and leather leggings.

'Thanks for coming in, Finn. I take it you're aware that we've got a bit of a situation.'

I slouch deeper. 'Situation? I was more going with clusterfuck.'

Without blinking, she pushes her tablet across the desk. The headlines slap me in the face.

LENNOX IN THREE-WAY SHAME WITH TORY MP'S FIANCÉE

PINK-HAIRED FLANKER FACES RED CARD AFTER ALPINE ANTICS

DOUBLE SNOW JOB FOR SCOTTISH RUGBY STAR

'Jesus,' I mutter, scrolling through. Stomach acid eats through my gut. 'They've been busy.'

'So have your sponsors. The car dealership pulled their offer for you this morning. And the Rebels' leadership demands a meeting first thing tomorrow.'

The walls of the office shrink inward.

'Look.' I pitch my weight forward. 'It was all consensual fun. Everyone was having a great time. I swear, I had no idea who they were.'

'That's actually worse.' There's a flash of disgust on her face. 'And the sisters angle?'

'*Step*sisters,' I correct. 'And no, I didn't know. It's not like I planned it. I hardly remember the details. Too bad, judging by these pictures. Looks like a proper belter.'

Now I get a rage-fuelled look, but she immediately reins it

in. Her face is the picture of neutral professionalism. You'd think she wasn't looking at human garbage.

Damn, she's good. That's why she's my agent.

'You're taking this well,' I say. 'I expected more...shouting.'

'Would shouting help?'

'Might feel more normal.' That and random smacks to the back of the head. My mother's MO.

She sighs loudly. 'Finn, I'm not angry. I'm disappointed.'

Uh oh.

'Aye, well. Get in line.' I scratch at a scab on my knuckle until it bleeds. 'So what's the plan? Sackcloth and ashes? Public flogging?'

'How about taking this seriously?'

'Fine. And then?'

'Not sure yet. Community service or charity, a fundraiser. Something that shows contrition without undermining our positioning.'

I nod, throat tight. 'And the Rebels?'

'I'm meeting with Coach Wallace later. Brodie's coming too.'

Great. Captain Perfect to the rescue.

'He's on your side, Finn,' she states, as if she could read my mind.

'Everyone's on my side until they're not.'

'Spare me the lost boy routine.'

The door opens again, and a woman walks in. Dark ponytail and a fringe cut with military precision. Deep red on lips that are too full to be fair. She looks like a pin-up who hasn't slept in a week and bleeds espresso. Curvy and vibrating with an energy that makes it hard not to stare. She has a glittery purple travel mug in one arm, a stack of papers in the other, and a step like she's marching into battle.

I sit up without meaning to.

'Sorry I'm late. Printer jammed again. We have a hate-hate

relationship.' She turns to me. 'Theo MacMickin. I don't believe we've met in person.'

Her eyes are violet-blue and sharp. Like they've already decided what I am. And whatever it is, they're not wrong.

'Finn Lennox. Professional cock-up.' I hold out a hand.

She sets the papers and mug down before taking it. Her grip is firm and no-nonsense. 'Professional rugby player who went off track. There's a difference.'

Something in my chest eases a wee bit.

'Theo's my assistant and our social media manager,' Charlie explains. 'She'll be handling your public rehabilitation.'

I'd let her handle plenty of things – if this were a different week, in a different life.

What? Calm doon, cowboy.

'Lucky her.'

Theo sits down next to me and crosses her legs. 'Let's be clear. I can help manage how the world sees you, but I can't change who you are. That part's on you.'

'Do you think I have to change who I am?'

'Do *you* think you have to?' She lifts a brow and slides a document toward me. 'This is your new schedule. Media blackout until I say otherwise, I'll handle your socials. Everything goes through me. Daily check-ins. We start tomorrow.'

Her gaze holds mine. Bright, unflinching, and too damn blue, measuring the gap between what I say and what I mean.

Charlie's phone lights up. She frowns, checks the screen, and stands. 'Give me a minute', she says, halfway to the door.

Theo glances after her, unreadable.

Family call? Feels like it. Or maybe she needed a break from me. Wouldn't blame her. Charlie's heels click away, and suddenly it's just me and the woman who's going to hold me hostage for the foreseeable future. The silence stretches thin as I count the bricks in the wall.

'So,' I say and stretch lazily, 'your name is Theo. Isn't that…a boy's name?'

'So, you slept with two women at the same time. Isn't that overcompensating?' Her voice is calm but cuts like a blade. 'Do you even *understand* the fallout of what you've done?'

I summon my practised smile. 'Gave two ladies a good time?'

Her cheeks light up with anger. It looks surprisingly cute.

'You've put this entire agency at risk. Charlie built this from nothing after her fiancé cheated on her and her own father took his side. And you—' She stops and inhales sharply through her nose. 'Your behaviour wasn't just reckless. It was selfish and childish!'

Air stalls behind my collarbone, and the words almost get stuck halfway up. 'I agree. And I'm sorry.'

'Do you? And are you? Because this isn't only about you. It's about Charlie. About every person who works here. Every client whose reputation gets tarnished by association. Not to mention your team.'

'I said I'm sorry.'

'Oh, I heard you. But honestly? You don't get to feel a bit sorry when other people are mopping up your mess.' She taps her pen against the paper, a rapid staccato. 'The Rebels might drop you. Did that occur to you?'

It has. Every waking minute since I sobered up. 'They won't, probably. They need me to play. I need to play.'

Her eyes stop flaring long enough to ask a question. 'Why weren't you answering any calls?'

My father's coffin flashes through my mind. What should I say? *Because of the man who left me as a child and died in prison and whose funeral I'm now skipping.* Saying that would sound like an excuse, and it's not.

'Forgot my charger, and my phone died.' Lie, obviously. Truth's heavier than that.

'For over a week?'

'I was busy.'

She gives me a once-over. 'Clearly.'

I lean towards her. 'Look, I was pished, awright? Fucking *gone*. First time in over a year, so excuse me if I couldn't handle the booze and lost the plot.'

'Why did you drink so much then?'

Charlie walks back in before I can answer. Saved by the bell.

'Sorry about that.' She sits down, all business again. 'That was MacKenzie Sporting. They are reconsidering all active contracts. The exact words were something along the lines of *"We pride ourselves on family values and expect the same from our partners and their associates".*'

Family values. Right. Because nothing says family values like dropping someone the minute they fuck up. I know that game all too well. That's what family is, right? My leg starts bouncing again. Can't help it.

I get it. They want squeaky clean reputations.

'Brodie's already fielding questions at the gym,' Charlie says. 'The press ambushed him this morning.'

Fuck. Brodie. Now he's caught in my mess, and that's the last thing he needs after getting out of his own pool of shite with the gambling and all that.

'Tell him I'm sorry.'

'Oh no. No, you'll tell him yourself and get the thrashing you deserve,' Charlie says.

Not that I want to. But I know I owe him.

Charlie's phone pings again, she glances at it and recoils. 'My father's seen the headlines. Now he's reminding me of my incompetence and awful decisions. Love how this year's starting.' She switches it off, tossing it on the desk.

A chill sluices down my spine. George Harrington, the legendary, ruthless London sports agent. I don't know the whole story, but I think he's still livid that his eldest daughter – heir to his empire – left his firm last year. I heard some stuff about him. People talk. And now I've given him ammunition. 'Charlie, I—'

'Don't worry about him.'

But I do. I've let her down. Let everyone down, not just myself.

I need to fix this.

I dig my fingers into my knees to stop the bobbing. The silence in Charlie's office feels like the hush before a eulogy. Fitting, since my career is apparently about to be buried on the same day as the man who fathered me.

'There *might* be a way forward.' Charlie breaks the quiet. She's staring at her laptop, scrolling through what must be an endless parade of my public humiliation. 'MacKenzie Sporting just emailed. They're willing to reconsider their position if – and I quote – "Mister Lennox demonstrates a visible commitment to personal growth and family values".'

I answer with a dry noise in my throat. 'What does that even mean? Should I grow a beard? Take up meditation? Ferment kombucha and get a puppy?'

'It means,' Theo cuts in, not looking up from her lists, 'they want to see you become less of a liability. They need reassurance you're not going to drag their brand through another tabloid scandal, frolicking with three influencers and a bottle of Wreck the Hoose Juice on a golf course.'

Charlie's eyes light up. 'All they need is proof you're trying. That you're committed. Stable and settled.'

Theo scoffs, a small sound that somehow fills the room. 'As if the likes of him ever settle.'

'But what if he *did*?' Charlie says, voice rising with excitement. 'When an athlete gets caught in a scandal, they often redeem themselves with a dependable partner. A wholesome girlfriend or love story. The public laps it up.'

I stare at her. 'Do you want me to lie? Pretend I'm suddenly madly in love?'

'That's the idea, yes,' Charlie says slowly.

'I hold someone's hand in public and pretend I've changed? Fuck me. That's bonkers. And also borderline blackmail.'

Charlie shakes her head. 'No, Finn. This is publicity. Of course, you're free to not do it. You have free will – but you might not have a team or a contract anymore. So, you need either a girlfriend or a time machine.' She lets out a ragged exhale. 'And I swear to God, if I lose this agency because of one man's dick…'

Okay, yeah. But… My voice nearly sticks in my throat. 'I never had a real girlfriend. That's a known fact. Nobody'd believe it.'

'They will if we sell it right.' Charlie braces her arms across her chest. 'Let's run with that idea for a minute. Let's say you didn't go on a hedonistic bender because you're a daftie – but because you were heartbroken. You had been dating in secret, she dumped you, then you spiralled. No cheating, that's important.' A shadow crosses her face. 'You were split up. But now you both realise what a terrible mistake you made. The public *loves* a grovelling man in emotional pain and a happily ever after.'

I shake my head. 'That's mental.'

'Wrong. It's brilliant,' Charlie insists. 'The rugby bad boy, humbled by true love. We sell the public the three Rs,' she explains. 'Regret – you didn't cheat, you were broken up. Reform – you're fixing yourself. Romance – you did it all because you thought you lost your one true love.'

Theo's pen stops moving. 'It could work.' Her tone stays cool and analytical. 'But we'd need the right woman. Someone credible and professional. Someone who doesn't get…caught up. Someone who balances out his…whatever *this* is.' She gestures vaguely in my direction.

'And who the hell would be insane enough to agree to that?' I ask, because I honestly have no idea. It's not like there's a 'fake girlfriend for hire'-agency. Or is there? Either way, I'm not interested. And if we can't find anyone, this bullshit idea might go away. I can sit it out.

The quiet stretches, taut as a pulled hamstring. Theo's eyes flick to Charlie, then to me. One beat, two.

'Me,' she says suddenly. 'I'll do it.'

Charlie turns her head sharply to stare at Theo.

My jaw drops. 'Wait. You?'

'Yes, me.' She meets my gaze head-on. 'I'm already handling your social media rehabilitation. This is merely an extension of that.'

'But—'

'I'm organised and reliable. The opposite of your type. Gives it a realistic edge.'

'My *type*?'

'Blonde, leggy, rich, famous, likes to party.' She ticks them off on her fingers. 'I'm none of those things.'

'I don't have a *type*,' I protest, but my eyes drift to her curves despite myself.

Not that I'd say it aloud, because I know better, but they painted curves like that on bomber planes in the Second World War.

'Are you serious about this?' Charlie's focus narrows to Theo's face.

'Deadly.' Theo adjusts her posture, subtle but exact. 'We can frame it as workplace romance. Happens all the time.' Now her gaze darkens for a second. 'It's the most logical and efficient solution. I'm familiar with the strategy and can control the narrative. Keep him in line.'

'Keep me in line?' I cough out a laugh. 'I'm not a dog.'

'True. Dogs can be trained.' Her gaze flicks over me. 'Consider it a professional arrangement, leash optional.'

'What's in it for you?' I watch her too closely and let her sense it.

Her shoulders lift a fraction, lips firming into a neutral line before she answers. 'Elite Edge's survival. My job, which I happen to really, really like.'

I lean back and take her in. The navy pencil skirt. The way she holds herself, spine straight, shoulders back.

Charlie clears her throat. 'This is…unexpected. But yeah, it might work. We can trust Theo. She's smart and capable with girl next door vibes.'

'And completely not my type,' I add with a wink. 'Your words, not mine.'

Theo's eyes frost over. 'Which makes it perfect.'

Perfect isn't the word I'd use. Insane, more like. 'So, you'll be my…*girlfriend*.'

'Your redemption arc and colleague,' she corrects. 'Nothing more. Nothing less.'

I study her face. Those full lips, the cool depth in her eyes. She's not afraid of me. Not impressed by me. And not interested in me at all.

The last one stings a bit, I have to admit.

'So, we're agreed?' Charlie taps a manicured nail against her phone. The tap-tap-tap grates on my already frayed nerves.

'Aye,' I mumble, even though 'agreed' is a vast understatement. More like reluctantly strapped to a rocket headed for Planet Awkward.

'Fab. We tell the team you fell in love at work and had been secretly seeing each other for a while before you briefly broke up. Needed to keep it quiet. Professional and personal reasons. Blah blah. The usual bollocks. The team needs to buy it,' Charlie explains and ignores my existential dread. 'Except… We have to tell Brodie. He can smell bullshit from a mile off, and no one in this room wants to incur his wrath when he does.'

I glance at Theo, who's busy making a list. Her fringe falls across her forehead, and she blows it aside with an impatient puff. Focussed and precise. Everything I'm not.

'Okay.' I tap a finger against my own knee, trying to match Charlie's irritating rhythm. 'And what exactly would that involve?'

Theo hands me a sheet of paper, bullet-pointed in meticulous handwriting. 'Only touching in public. Kissing is acceptable, but no tongues.'

Charlie coughs into her fist.

Kissing Theo? The thought lights up the part of me that never learns, a mix of panic and...intrigue, perhaps. Or the lingering aftertaste of last week's debauchery. Who can tell?

'Social media posts,' she continues. 'Photos of us together. Casual dates. Just enough to...'

'...convince the world I'm not a self-destructive sexaholic?' I finish for her.

She nods. 'Aye. I'll create a schedule of appearances. This is *strictly* performative and professional.'

No one speaks. The space between us turns dense enough to feel. Theo watches me, those violet-blue eyes searching for the catch, the angle, the hidden play.

I let out a defeated sigh. 'How long will this charade last?'

'Until the season ends in May, so roughly five months,' Charlie says, fingers steepled under her chin. 'With my luck, I'm sure that by then, some other player will have screwed up royally. And you two can have a civilised, amicable, quiet split.'

'We go our separate ways,' Theo says. 'No hard feelings. No messy breakup. Just...puff and gone.'

Puff and gone. As if whatever shred of reputation I might've had hadn't already puffed and gone in a cloud of champagne and glitter.

Five months of pretending to be someone I'm not. With someone who's the exact opposite of...well, everyone I've ever been with, myself included.

But then I think of the exhaustion etched around Charlie's eyes. How her words wobbled when she mentioned her father. Of Brodie, catching flak at the gym. The Rebels, the lads who've become my family in the past eight months since the team's formation.

'Fine,' I say, tighter than I mean. 'I'll survive five months.'

Not for the optics or for the sponsors or even for myself. But for them, for Charlie and Theo and the team. I'm not in Glasgow today to bury my father. But I might be burying the part of me he made. For the first time in my life, I'm trying to do the right thing.

I'm going to lie through my teeth.

But for a good cause. My redemption and my career, Charlie's agency, Theo's job.

'Awright, Miss MacMickin,' I say, 'Let's see how you turn me into boyfriend material.'

Chapter 3

Theo

Finn's hands are beautiful. He's spinning my pen between fingers that shouldn't be that graceful. Lean and dexterous. His hands are strong, tanned, inked to hell, and topped with nails neat enough to suggest serious self-care. There's a scar across his knuckle and a skull on his middle finger that's so poorly drawn it could pass for a cartoon bean. And still, somehow, it all fits.

Of course, I'm only staring because I'm assessing the right photo angle. That's why we're here past eight on a Monday night, after everyone's gone. The press release two days ago was the launch of *Operation Dummy Pass*.

I scoop the printed lists off my desk. On top is the final version of our statement:

Following recent speculation, we wish to provide context around events involving Finn Lennox.

Mr Lennox experienced a breach of privacy when footage of a private encounter was circulated online without his knowledge or consent. At the time of the incident, Mr Lennox was not aware of the identities of the two individuals involved.

The material was recorded without permission and released unlawfully.

In the weeks prior to this event, Mr Lennox was navigating the breakdown of a personal relationship. The emotional fallout from that situation contributed directly to a period of instability and poor decision-making.

'I am deeply sorry and take full responsibility for my actions. I let down my team, my supporters, and the people who believed in me. I was dealing with something personal, but that is no excuse. I have work to do to earn back the trust I lost. And I will.'

The relationship in question has since been resumed. The decision to move forward together was not made lightly. It reflects mutual accountability, personal growth, and a shared commitment to rebuilding with intention.

No further comments will be made at this time.

That was the first step to create the illusion of our whirlwind workplace romance – the rugby star and the girl who takes his pictures. I almost scoff. Now comes step number two: a cosy-couply picture for social media. My expertise.

I position the ring light. The white-washed brick wall behind us provides perfect contrast. My phone's camera settings are optimised. Everything's ready – except for the two leads in this romantic charade.

'Listen.' I level the tripod for the last time. 'This should be simple. Stand next to me and hold my hand.'

He moves slowly, as if he knows how not-simple this is. Then he offers his hand, palm up.

I place mine into his – and we both freeze.

His hand swallows mine whole. Warm and callused. There's a small thrum under my skin, a warning signal.

It's just a hand. Just a hand.

'Christ, this feels weird,' he says.

'No argument there. But it's meant to look natural. Not

whatever *this* is. We look like we're hostages, desperately holding on to each other until the polis arrive.'

He frowns. 'Kind of fitting.'

'Finlay, please relax your shoulders.'

'They *are* relaxed, Theodora.'

'They're practically touching your ears. And you're crushing my bones.' I yank my hand free. The blood rushes back and I still feel the imprint of his grip. I shake it off. 'Let's try a close-up instead. Just our hands on the desk. Give me your jumper.'

Finn raises a questioning eyebrow. 'You want me to strip, just say so.'

'I need a backdrop, daftie.'

He shrugs it off, slow and unbothered, the black hoodie dragging the white T-shirt across his chest. The cotton pulls over muscle. Broad shoulders, defined arms, every inch of him cut and hot and completely unfair. His tattoos catch the light, ink winding down his arm. Veins shift under the skin as he moves.

I shouldn't be watching this closely.

He hands me the jumper.

A pulse kicks between my legs, immediate and mortifying.

Dammit. What is it about tattooed men in white tees?

I exhale through my nose and smooth the hoodie across the desk surface. 'Place your hand here, palm down.'

Finn complies and I position my hand over his, fingers barely touching.

'It's supposed to look artistic.' I snap a test shot, check the screen, and grimace. The overhead perspective highlights his knuckle ink in stark detail.

'Your tattoos are problematic.'

'You're only noticing that now?'

'I mean especially for family-friendly photography purposes.'

The F-U-C-K across the knuckles of his right hand stares

back at me in bold black letters. My red polka-dot nails sit absurdly cheerful against it.

'It stands for Focus, Unity, Courage, and Kindness,' he says.

'Aye, right. And Theo stands for Tequila, Handcuffs, Ecstasy, and Orgies.'

He laughs. A full-bodied, head-tipped-back, no-performance laugh rips out of him as if his body couldn't stop it if it tried. The sound is so deep and rich, I feel it in my chest first, then lower. A tingle I don't have time for.

His laugh ebbs out slowly, but the sound lingers. So does the heat in the space between us.

He moves closer, only an inch or so. 'Your hands are small.'

Of course he'd notice my proportion problem. They *are* small and have always made me feel slightly unfinished. 'I know, it's a bit weird. But also irrelevant.'

'Naw, not weird. I like girls with small hands.' He pauses and holds my gaze, bold as brass. 'It makes my dick look bigger.'

What comes out of me isn't a laugh. It's a giggle-grunt. Sharp, breathy, undignified. The sound of my guard tripping over itself and face-planting right in front of him.

Deflect, deflect!

'Judging by the screenshots I saw, that's not a real issue. So stop swanning about and focus.' I force myself to breathe calmly and adjust the angle again. 'Can you tuck your thumb in?'

He grins and shifts his grip without comment. But now our hands lie limp like two dead fish at a market stall.

'Ugh. This isn't working.' I jab at delete with more force than necessary like it's the phone's fault. 'We need something that says, "besotted couple" not "business transaction".'

'Isn't that what this is?'

'Yes, but it can't appear that way.' I pat my phone against

my palm a few times. 'The sponsors need to believe you're reformed through the power of…my stabilising influence.'

Finn's mouth quirks. 'Your stabilising influence. Listen to yourself.'

'Got a better idea?'

He sinks back, arms folded. 'Several, but none you'd approve of.'

Don't blush.

Too late, my traitorous face goes full cherry tomato. 'Please concentrate, Finn.'

'I am concentrating. You're the one overthinking this.'

I glare at him. 'I'm not overthinking. It just seems that way next to the mess you're in from chronically *underthinking*.'

'Maybe. But I look great in it.'

He's enjoying this. I can tell by the smug tilt of his mouth. He's reading me – my flush, my glare, the tiny ways I lose control – and cataloguing every reaction. I don't know why that's riling me up so much, but it is.

I press my fingers to my temples. 'Our hands need to tell a story. This looks like we've never touched each other before.'

'We haven't.' There's a glint in his light blue eyes like he's about to steal something just to see if I'll chase him.

'Fine. New approach,' I say. 'We'll sit on the chair.'

'It's too small for both of us.'

'I'll perch on your knee, of course. Seriously, does getting hit by human battering rams for a living impair your cognitive abilities this much?'

'Ouch.'

I hear myself too late. I didn't mean to sound this bitchy. That's not who I am. 'Sorry, Finn. That was uncalled for.'

'Forgiven. You're cute when you're all ruffled and bossy.'

Unhelpful observation: compliments from self-serving numpties still register.

I drag the chair into position. 'Sit,' I command, pointing at it like I'm directing a disobedient labrador.

Finn angles his head just enough to make room for doubt but complies, dropping into my office chair with casual grace. His knees splay wide, taking up space in that uniquely male way that screams territorial dominance.

Of course he's a man spreader. But to be fair, there's a lot of man to spread in his case.

MacMickin, stop!

'Now what?' he asks.

'Now I sit and we look besotted. It's what couples do.' I smooth my skirt. 'Nothing personal, only a job.'

'Sure. No one's enjoying this.'

I position myself on his right thigh, perched at the edge, maintaining maximum distance. Spine locked, shoulders on high alert. I'm *technically* sitting. Emotionally? Mid-exit.

One of his thighs is enough to serve as an ottoman.

'You know, you're surprisingly uncomfortable with physical contact,' he murmurs from behind.

'I'm not uncomfortable. I'm professional.'

'There's a difference between professional and rigid.'

'There's also a difference between relaxed and inappropriate,' I counter.

I shouldn't care what he thinks. Yet something about his observation needles me. Am I rigid? Perhaps. But rigid has kept me safe when everything else crumbled.

'Relax, List Girl.'

I sigh and scoot back, letting my weight settle. His thigh is… Jesus. Solid and unreasonably comfortable. The muscle beneath me tenses, like he's bracing on instinct. For stability, probably.

Completely normal. Totally fine.

It's just a leg. A giant, irritatingly perfect leg that feels like it was sculpted for this situation. His thigh's all heat and muscle, hard and thick. I know the rest of him is also… I mean, I've seen the photos. Oh my god. I can't believe I'm thinking about his…equipment. Here. Now.

The seam of my tights drags in just the wrong spot. I reposition again, but that only makes things worse.

I am never mentioning this to anyone. Ever.

'Better?' I ask and my voice sounds a tad wobbly.

'Getting there.' His breath strokes the side of my neck. 'Put your hand on your knee.'

I place my hand on my left knee, palm up. Finn covers it with his own, fingers curling naturally around mine. His thumb rests against my wrist, where my pulse quickens for no reason.

'Now look at our hands,' he instructs, voice lower than before.

I do. His large hand, tanned and inked, cradling my smaller one with its red nails. We strike the right note between intimate and protective. Most importantly: convincing.

He moves his thumb, slowly stroking back and forth across the pulse point below my palm. The contact is featherlight, but it sends a jolt up my arm, straight to somewhere I pretend isn't reacting.

'What are you doing, Finn?'

'Making it seem real. That's the goal, right?'

His thumb continues its path, tracing invisible patterns. This feels intimate in ways it definitely shouldn't. And I'm beginning to understand how rows of women end up in bed with him. At the same time.

Thank God I'm not one of them.

I lift my phone and take pictures. Click. Click. Hands, framed like a stock image. Romantic intimacy, brought to you by strategic discomfort. I check the preview. Our intertwined hands fill the frame.

'Got it?'

'Nearly.' I take three more shots, then scroll through the photos. They're perfect. Intimate without being showy. The kind of casual affection that can't be faked.

Except we just did.

I start to pull away, but he tightens his fingers slightly around my hand.

'Theo.'

'What?'

'Thank you. For doing this.' His voice is different. No more swagger or deflection.

I tip my chin half a notch, and he's watching me. His pink hair catches the ring light, bright enough to hurt if I stare too long. But his eyes are serious and grateful. I did *not* expect that.

'Don't worry about it, Finn. That's my job.'

'No, it's not. Your job is social media and being an assistant. This is… I don't know. A sacrifice?'

The back of my neck burns. 'I want to keep this job. No, I *have* to keep this job. It's all I've got, and I didn't lie when I said that I love it.'

His thumb still strokes across my pulse, and I realise he's been doing it unconsciously all the time.

'I think you might work too hard, Theo.'

'Someone has to keep this place running,' I retort, trying to regain my composure. 'Especially when certain rugby players are busy creating international incidents and incriminating headlines.'

He winces. 'I messed up. I know that.'

I glance up and find him not smirking for once. 'Yes, you did. But we'll fix this mess.' His hand lets go, and I stand up to put distance between us. I rub my palm on my skirt, but the warmth stays exactly where he left it. 'I…erm…should edit these.'

'Course.'

I lean against my desk and busy myself with my phone, cropping and filtering. Finn stays quiet in the chair, man spreading away, as I work.

'What's the caption?' he asks.

Rucked Up Ruse

'I was thinking... How about "Turns out, even I can't fuck everything up"?'

'Aye, sounds like me.'

'Hashtag secondchance.'

He laughs. 'You could probably rebrand Satan.'

'Isn't that what I'm already doing?' I busy myself by packing away the ring light. 'Okay, we stick to the plan. Small doses of public affection. Build the story gradually.'

'Gradually, huh?' He gets up and stretches, arms behind his head, his slow, self-satisfied grin built to rile me up. 'Cool. Just let me know when it gets too much for you. Wouldn't want you blushing through the whole thing.'

Then he saunters off.

And my face? A raging tomato again.

Chapter 4

Finn

I catch the ball with my skull.
It bounces off my head with a dull thud, then skitters across the grass like it's running away from my incompetence. Not my finest moment.

'Fucking hell, Lennox!' Brodie bellows. 'That was aimed at your hands, not your pretty face.'

The cold air bites at my cheeks. It's our first full-pitch session outside since the holiday break, before the first game of the year on the tenth. The reporters on the touchline are a reminder that my life's turned into a soap opera. But I'm here to play rugby, not star in *Coronation Street*. They point their lenses like snipers. I want to flip them the bird, but I keep the urge on a leash.

I'm a respectable man now, apparently.

I wipe mud from my face. 'Sun was in my eyes.'

'It's fucking Scotland in January,' Scottie Kerr shouts from the other side. The Rebels' centre, my flatmate, and a gobshite. 'There's nae sun. Just admit you're distracted by thoughts of your *wee girlfriend*.'

Snickers ripple through the lads. They've been at it ever since the post went live last night. The press release and the

Rucked Up Ruse

social campaign are supposed to steer the public perception from 'reckless serial shagger' to 'heartbroken man making a mistake'. But the team doesn't care about narratives. They care about a good laugh and taking the piss. Can't blame them.

'Aye, Finn, what's it like having a woman who knows what a book is?' Scottie shouts, his grin wide enough to split his face.

'Probably too much thinking for him.' Our Number 8, James MacKenna adjusts his scrum cap. He's usually quiet, but even he's getting in on the act.

A few minutes later, the ball – a white and neon green blur – glances off my chest and drops. Again.

'Lennox!' Coach Wallace barks my name through the chill. 'You want to play or piss about?'

He's right. My body's here, but my brain's hooked on dark hair in a high ponytail and rules I'm not sure I fully understand. It's with a pair of bossy blues that pin me down without trying. With the press of her round arse against my thigh, that soft weight when she settled in.

Don't even dream about it.

We run the drill again. This time I'm locked in, body moving on muscle memory. Catch, pass, sprint. Repeat. Rugby's simple when you strip away the noise. Has always been that way for me. It's the rest of life that's complicated.

Scottie sidles up during water break, sweat dripping from his forehead. 'Still weird I've never seen that Elite Edge girl around. You've been hiding her under the bed, or what?'

I take a long swig to gather my thoughts. 'We've been keeping it quiet, that's all.'

'That why you were shagging two birds in Switzerland?'

I splutter. 'We were…on a break.'

'A break?' Connor Duff pipes up from behind. He's a winger with zero filter. 'That the one where you broke your dick trying to handle two at once?'

The water bottle crumples in my grip. 'Fuck off, Duffy Duck.'

'Seriously though,' Scottie presses, 'how'd you land her?'

'What can I say?' I shrug, aiming for nonchalant. 'She loves my natural charm.'

'And your ability to multitask,' Scottie shoots back, dry as toast.

More laughter. Brodie, standing a few yards away, shoots me a glare that could freeze lava, then shakes his head. He's been silent about it all, which is almost worse than the constant ribbing. He's in on it, that's why. But that doesn't mean he approves.

The reporters hovering just beyond the railings are still watching us like hawks, vultures, whatever predatory bird fits. I flip my bottle and catch it, still giving them nothing. It's not easy.

'Must be stressful, though,' Connor muses, 'trying to keep track of which bits go where. Like playing Twister but naked.'

'And with extra parts,' Scottie adds. 'Sounds exhausting. I get tired just imagining it.'

Coach's whistle cuts through the banter. 'Move!'

We jog back to position. My thighs burn from yesterday's gym session, but it's nothing compared to the burn in my face. I used to dish it out; now I'm the punch-line.

Doesn't feel great, to be honest.

The drill starts. I focus on the ball, the grass, the space. Not on her serious expression when she laid out the 'rules' of our so-called relationship. Not on the giggle that escaped her when I made that joke. Not on how electric her hand felt in mine or how her pulse jumped when I touched her.

And not that cute rosy flare that I can't wait to see again.

The ball sails over my head.

'Fuck's sake!' Coach roars. 'Get your head out of her lap and on the ball, Lennox!'

The team erupts in laughter.

Rucked Up Ruse

I blow them a kiss, and I'm grinning, but they don't know what happened, how fucked up it all is. And I intend to keep it that way.

Eventually Coach makes us run suicides. Sprint. Touch the line. Turn. Again. And again. Lungs burning, legs screaming, sweat pouring down my back. By the end, I'm ready to collapse.

'That was a shite session, lads,' Wallace says. 'Hit the showers. Lennox, a word.'

The others trudge off. Coach waits until we're alone. 'You with us, Finn?'

'As I said last week during the crisis meeting, one hundred per cent, Coach.'

'Because your head seems to be elsewhere.' He folds his arms. 'Management's watching you. You've used up all your favours, Lennox. One more fuck-up and even I can't save you. Don't make me regret backing you.'

My mouth goes dry. 'I know. And I won't.'

'Good.' He claps my shoulder and walks away.

The reporters start shouting questions, but I ignore them, heading for the changing room to get my stuff. Won't make it into the shower, though. Because it's almost time.

Right on schedule, a mint green Fiat 500 putters up to the kerb, looking like it escaped from a children's cartoon. Theo's car, exactly where her plan said it would be. In another life, she'd have made an excellent bank robber. The photographers lurking by the fence perk up.

'That your girlfriend's ride?' Connor grins, shouldering his gear bag. 'Seems like a Tic Tac.'

This is it. Our first public appearance as a 'couple'. Lenses twitch and flash, hungry for the show we're about to give them.

'Hope she brought your juice box and colouring book.' Connor laughs at his own joke.

Each step toward her car loads my calves with sand. It's the cameras making me nervous, I keep telling myself, not Theo. Definitely not the fact I'm about to kiss her in public for the first time. Professionally and all that.

Through the windscreen, I spot her fussing with her ponytail. Her fringe sits perfectly straight across her forehead. Her coat's the kind of green that makes her pale skin glow. It's true that I don't have a type, I love them in all sizes and shapes. But damn, she draws the eye – whether she means to or not – and I keep noticing details I normally wouldn't.

The car door opens, and she steps out. Those serious blue eyes scan the scene, clocking the reporters, my teammates, the choreography of this moment.

'Hi, *babe*,' she says with a beaming smile, loud enough for the nearest paps to hear.

'Hey…you.' The two words rumble out rough in a way I didn't plan.

We're one foot apart. Close enough to catch the trace of sweat cooling behind her ear, sweetened by whatever body wash she uses. Skin-soft and fresh. It hits low. Blood, focus – all rushing south.

Theo looks flustered underneath her pro-facade, colour striping up her neck again.

As I said, really fucking cute.

I guess I should kiss her, that's what boyfriends do. A quick peck to sell this show. But my legs freeze and my brain shorts out. Why am I suddenly paralysed by the thought of pressing my lips to a woman's cheek?

Theo takes control. Her small hand cups my jaw, warm against my cold skin. She rises on her toes and presses her lips to the corner of my mouth.

Soft. So fucking soft.

My knees buckle slightly. I breathe her in too deeply –

Rucked Up Ruse

vanilla and cherries and whatever witchy thing melts all consonants off my tongue. I find her waist instinctively and hold her, steadying us both. For a second, everything stills. Just her mouth near mine. Her fingers warm on my face. My whole body tight with the ache not to fuck this up.

'You reek of PE kit in a Lidl bag', she whispers against my cheek, still smiling for our audience.

The cameras click frantically.

I let out a rough chuckle, and it's unguarded. 'I thought you'd love my natural musk.'

'Get in the car, skunk. And for the love of God, open the window.'

I fold into the passenger seat, a process that requires more leg origami than expected. My knees practically touch my nose.

'This thing's tiny,' I grumble as she climbs in behind the wheel. 'Do you keep the other half at home?'

'Not everyone needs to compensate with vehicle size or horse power.' She starts the engine, which wheezes like an asthmatic kitten.

'You insulting my manhood, MacMickin?'

'Obviously not. Just a general commentary on athletes and cars.' She pulls away from the kerb, waving at the photographers. Once we're out of sight, the smile drains from her face. 'That should give them something to write about for now.'

I adjust my seat, trying to find a position where my knees aren't jammed against the dashboard. 'Think they bought it?'

'Guess so.' She keeps her eyes on the road. 'Though next time, try not to look like I'm holding a knife to your throat.'

'Next time...when's that again?'

'We have a dinner reservation this weekend. Big date night.'

'Ah, right. The schedule.' I scrub a hand over my face. 'You always this organised with your boyfriends?' It's such a cheap attempt at prying that it almost makes me laugh out loud about myself.

'You're explicitly not my boyfriend.'

Of course she's too smart to take the bait.

'I know. Just the lad you're snogging in car parks.'

Her hands tighten around the steering wheel. 'That wasn't a snog. That was merely a peck.'

'Tell that to my dick.'

She swerves slightly. 'Excuse me?'

'Kidding! Christ, woman, you'll kill us both.'

A small smile tugs at her lips. 'Stop shitting yourself. I have a wee car, but I'm a confident and competent driver.'

Who got deliciously rattled by my very inappropriate comment. I press my lips together to hide my grin and stare out of the window. 'So where are we going?'

'Your place first. You're screaming for a shower. Then we're meeting Charlie at the Sin & Tonic to go over the interview strategy.'

'All work and no play, MacMickin.'

She swings the car into the next turn like she's aiming to test the airbags. 'Unlike you, I take my job seriously. You should try it some time.'

We drive in silence for a while. The sort that makes you notice your own heartbeat, lets your mind wander, and conjures up unwanted memories. A slamming door. A phone that never rings. A man I stopped calling 'dad' long before he died.

Nope. Not going there.

I roll my neck and watch Duncraig's houses blur past.

Her phone shuffles some old pop song I don't recognise. Girl voices with syrupy harmonies. So that's her vibe? Interesting.

'Who's this?'

'The Shangri-Las.'

'Sounds like a girl gang with matching eyeliner.'

'Pretty much.' Theo lets another real smile sneak in as she drums her fingers on the steering wheel in time with the song. 'So... Your teammates seem okay.'

'Och, they tolerate me.'

'Because you're such an amazing flanker?' she quips with faux awe.

'That's for them and Coach to decide. But I know that I'm good, aye.'

I glance at her profile. The determined set of her jaw, the slight furrow between her brows, and the lifting tip of her nose. 'You kissed me in front of all of them and the press, Theo. That's gutsy.'

'As I said, it was hardly a kiss.' She sighs. 'Oh, boy. This is going to be tougher than I thought.'

'C'mon. It could be worse. You could be stuck with Scottie. He farts in his sleep.'

That startles a laugh out of her. It's a good sound. Good against dark memories. And I want to hear more of it.

'I got the one who only makes a tit of himself when he's awake. A real treat.'

I grin despite myself. And I got a feisty wee girlfriend.

Chapter 5

Theo

There are worse people to fake-date I guess.

Finn takes my coat with a little bow like he's auditioning for *Downton Abbey*. I roll my eyes, but I can't help the smile that sneaks in. I'm trying not to drop my clutch while we're performing our perfectly-faked, lovey-dovey reunion date.

Then he shrugs off his own coat and—

Oh.

Right.

That's *not* what I expected.

I mean, I've seen him shirtless a lot. He's half-naked in most of his Instagram photos, thirst-trapping it hard. But this is worse. It's not so much his white, crisp, annoyingly well-fitted shirt. It's the contrast. The pink hair. The tattoos creeping past his rolled-up sleeves. His tailored, navy trousers *and* the Air Jordans. He looks intentional. A man who draws attention with purpose.

Finn is making an effort for *Operation Dummy Pass*, and I'm oddly proud.

To be fair, I am, too. I'm wearing the black polka-dot

wiggle dress I bought in a vintage shop in London. Sweetheart neckline, cap sleeves, cinched waist. Cute, but comfortable. Nice, but not over the top.

'Shall we?' He presses a hand to the base of my spine.

It's barely a touch, nothing but soft pressure. I bite down on the reaction and lock it behind my teeth. My shoulders stay squared. As if that'll stop the flutter in my stomach.

Keep it together, MacMickin. Smile. Reinforce the illusion you're head over block heels in love with a walking snack in trainers. How hard can it be?

He leans in a little, close enough to brush my hair as he murmurs, 'You alright?'

No. Not really. He shouldn't clean up this well. Or smell that way – fresh cotton, orange peel, clean skin. Sharp enough to catch in my throat, heady enough to make me want to lean closer.

'Yeah, sure. I'm fine.' I force a smile, and focus on the lighting, the flowers, the glasses on the tables. Not how my skin is on fire where he touches me.

The maître d' leads us to a corner table with a view of the entire restaurant. Perfect for visibility without making it obvious we want to be seen. Good choice.

Finn pulls out my chair. I sit, say 'thank you', and wonder if I've entered a parallel universe where rogue rugby players have manners.

He sits across from me, stretching his legs long under the table. One foot brushes mine. On purpose, no doubt.

'Just so you're aware, we're being watched,' I mutter behind the menu.

'We're always being watched.' His mouth curves, smug as sin. 'That's the plan, right? So go on then, give them a show.'

I peek over my menu and clock the photographer planted two tables away to the side, sipping still water like it's vintage wine. 'Charlie should've hired someone less obvious.'

'You're adorable when you pretend this is your first rodeo.'

'And you're annoying when you pretend it's not.'

'Touché, chérie. Champagne?'

'I'm more of a fizzy orange-juice kinda gal.' I smooth the napkin across my lap.

'Noted.' He winks at the waiter. 'One Fanta for my… erm…girlfriend, and I'll take a ginger beer. Cheers.'

'Careful not to choke on that word,' I say over the rim of the menu. 'I'm not qualified to perform a Heimlich.'

Seriously, his lopsided, cocky grin should come with a warning label. Reckless, lit from somewhere deep, and aimed squarely at my better judgement. My insides sway off-centre. It's probably the pressure of playing a part I didn't rehearse properly. My nervous system's responding to environmental stressors, not the man in front of me. No matter how distractingly gorgeous his face might be when he decides to turn on the charm.

The waiter returns with our drinks and Finn raises his glass. 'To convincing performances. I mean…to true love.'

I clink my glass against his. 'To not making arses of ourselves.'

'Making an arse of myself is my speciality.'

'So I've gathered from your highlight reel.'

He flashes that maddening half-smile again. 'Which part impressed you most?'

'The unicorn onesie at the press conference was inspired.'

'Ah, a classic.' He sips his drink, mockingly lifting his little finger away from it. 'It's my favourite animal. Wait till you see the matching sleeping mask.'

I bite back a smile, but it slips out sideways anyway. 'I didn't expect anything less.'

I scan the menu, conscious of the photographer who keeps glancing our way, holding her phone up. 'What are you having?'

'Probably something separate,' he says, browsing the options. 'Can't stand when my food touches.'

I lower my menu. 'You're joking.'

'No. There are rules. Each veggie stays in its lane. Unless it's a stew, a soup, or a lasagne. I'd never joke about food boundaries. I'm not a monster.'

I blink. 'No, I mean... I'm the same. I use those sectioned plates at home.'

Surprise flashes in his eyes. 'The plastic ones with the little barriers?'

'Mine are ceramic, thank you very much. But yes.'

His grin turns triumphant. 'Look at us, we're like soul*plates*.'

'Pipe down, Lennox.' But I smile, unsure if him being funny puts me at ease or in danger.

Talking to Finn is easy. I keep waiting for the moment I'll have to carry the conversation, but it never comes. His company is comfortable, which *should* make me suspicious. My brain *should* be pinging alarms. Instead, it kicks up its feet, and folds its arms behind its head.

The waiter floats over and launches into the specials like he's announcing another royal birth. I nod along, half-listening. Finn orders the lasagne with garlic bread, I take the Scottish sirloin of beef burger.

Once the waiter leaves, Finn eases back in his chair. 'So, Theodora MacMickin. Tell me something real. Since we're going steady, I figure I should know more about you. How did you grow up?'

That's a question that sounds harmless unless you understand what the answer can cost. A knock on a door that I'd rather keep closed. But he's right, we need to know *something* about each other. Luckily, something is not everything and I can work with that.

'Fife, a coastal village called Elie.'

'Bit boring, then?'

'Kind of.' I take a sip of my drink. 'My dad was in the Royal Navy and was away a lot before he retired last year. Mum is a sculptor. Middle class, I suppose.'

'Sounds sheltered and cosy.'

'Parts were. But not all of it.' I twirl my glass and swallow the bitter taste that comes with remembering an absent father and a mother who couldn't get out of bed most days. 'What about you? Glasgow, right?'

'Aye. Easterhouse.'

I know enough to recognise that's not the easiest place to grow up. A place people have opinions about without ever setting foot there. 'What was that like?'

'Let's call it character building.' There's a smile, but it lands late. As if he had to pull it on by the collar. 'Learned to run fast early on. Came in handy for rugby.'

'Your parents?'

'My…biological father wasn't around. Not that it was a loss. My maw worked her arse off and had her hands full with my two older sisters.' He shrugs, casual, but his hand stays frozen tightly around the glass. 'Not much to tell.'

'Everyone has stories.'

'Some aren't worth sharing.'

His deflection is smooth and practised. I've used it myself. Keep it light, reveal nothing. Makes you wonder, doesn't it?

'What were you like at school?' I ask, to change the subject and perhaps level the field.

'Suspended a lot. I was a wee gobshite.' He laughs. 'Didn't like sitting still. Didn't like being told what to do.'

'Sounds like you.'

The food arrives, plates set down between us. Finn lounges in his chair with the casual confidence of someone who knows what he looks like, with the sharp-edged bone structure to back it up. Honestly, his face is unfair, that's the only word for it. Masculine to the point that makes it hard to keep your eyes away. Lines softened by a mouth that probably gets him into and out of trouble more than it should. Baby-blue eyes under long lashes. That's a face that gets away with things all the time.

And I'm not thrilled that it's working on me.

We eat in silence for a bit. Not awkward, but not easy either. I think I'm starting to see the man behind the front.

'So,' Finn says after a few bites, 'what made you work with Charlie?'

'I needed a fresh start.' My gaze drops before I pull it back up. 'London wasn't working out, neither professionally nor personally.'

'Ah, bad breakup?'

I flinch. 'Something like that.'

'Who'd leave you? Fuck that guy.'

I sit back in my chair, not far, but enough to mark distance, and adjust the napkin in my lap. 'What makes you think I wasn't the problem?'

'Because you're sitting here on your Saturday night, helping me fix my mess.' He points his fork at me. 'You're a fixer, not a breaker. You care.'

I don't have anything to say to that. It's oddly perceptive, and it catches me off guard.

'Sorry,' he says. 'Too much?'

'No, a bit unexpected.'

'I'm full of surprises, darlin'.' He smiles, and it's miles apart from the charm he flashes for cameras or the cheeky trademark grin.

I'm ready with a sarcastic reply, but it never makes it out. Not when he smiles at me in a way that triggers a full cranial vasodilation response, which is the scientific term for what happens when your face glows like a traffic light.

As I said, debilitating.

'Your turn again,' I say quickly. 'Why rugby? It looks like it hurts a lot.'

His smile morphs into a grin. 'It does. But I had to channel my ang—…energy somewhere.' He pushes his fork through the lasagne with a little too much focus. 'My PE teacher shoved me into this Active Schools thing when I was nine. Coach there said I had legs and no fear, and sent me to a club team. Told me to show up and not fuck it.'

'And did you?'

He gestures to himself. 'Here I am, in all my glory. I fuck up everything else, but never rugby.'

'There's more to it than that.'

He pauses, fork halfway to his mouth. 'Maybe. But that's for the second fake date, don't you think?'

He's hiding something. Not just the usual deflection, but something deeper. It's in the careful way he constructs each answer, revealing just enough to satisfy without exposing anything real.

It scratches at my curiosity. And that's dangerous.

'Fine,' I say. 'But I'm onto you, Lennox.'

'I bet.' He reaches across the table and takes my hand, his thumb tracing circles on my palm. 'The photographer got her phone out again.'

His skin is warm, rough in places. Every slow pass of his thumb drags awareness across my skin. I don't get how someone built to break through walls can touch like this. But I let him.

'You're good at this,' I admit.

'So are you.' His eyes meet mine. They're bright and disarmingly direct. No smirk, no shield. He sees more than I want him to, and he doesn't look away.

There's that flutter again.

Because I wasn't talking about being good at faking it. I was talking about the touching part. He's an absolute genius at that.

Woah. This is only to save Elite Edge and Charlie. The job I love, I remind myself. A sacrifice, as he called it. But as I intertwine my fingers with his, the part of me that's meant to stay untouched doesn't feel so untouched anymore.

I'm in control. I've got this.

And if I keep thinking it, I might even believe it.

Chapter 6

Finn

Dinner's almost over, and I've forgotten most of what I ate. Theo's small hand fits into mine, fingers interlocked as if we've done this a hundred times before. Only we haven't, and I've got no business noticing how soft her palm is. Or how my thumb keeps circling in a quiet rhythm, because I don't want to stop.

She's sitting opposite me, perfectly poised and composed. There's a tension in her hand. Not resistance, more alertness. And her pulse kicks against my fingertips.

This should be easy. Hold hands, smile for the camera, sell the illusion. I've done far worse for a lot less. But this feels different. *She* feels different. She curls her fingers against mine, giving me permission one breath at a time, and that rattles me more than if she'd giggled and leaned in with her tits out.

Theo MacMickin is a mystery. Tight smile, calm voice. But the second she talked about her family, she dropped her eyes like the words weighed too much. Said 'Elie' as if it wasn't worth remembering. I know what it sounds like when someone skips over the worst parts. I've been doing it my whole life.

Rucked Up Ruse

She hands over puzzle pieces one at a time, and I want the full picture.

I'd tried to throw her off with jokes and cheek, but she never missed a beat. She's smart. Scarily smart. The way she watched me when I laughed, as if she was filing it away for future reference. And I've got the sneaking suspicion she's hiding something. Not scandal-hiding, not my kind of hiding. But as if the reason she's so contained is that she's spent years building that armour.

The way she didn't deny the breakup, only flinched. And that flinch did things to me. Things that make no sense, because we're fake. A limited-time offer with full returns and no emotional repercussions. And yet I'm trying to decode the story behind one blink-and-you'll-miss-it moment. The old me wouldn't have noticed. Would've clocked the dress, the legs, the mouth, and skipped the small talk. But I want to know what happened to her. She's dressing it up, but the hurt is obvious.

I want to know who broke her so I can break him.

And why she still looks like she's trying to tape the pieces back together in silence.

Am I staring? Yeah. I should stop.

But…God, those lips.

Red as a fuck-you. Her top lip has a natural dip. I keep wondering what she tastes like. How long she'd let me kiss her before she pulled away.

Before I could mess it up.

Cause that's what I do.

A waitress places the bowl between us with a smile that lingers a tad too long on our hands. I don't let go.

Cranachan. Berries bleeding into cream, oats, whisky, honey, and one of those sugar shards stuck on top.

'One dessert.' I nod at it. 'Suppose we share?'

'Of course.' She blinks slowly. 'For the photos.'

'It's what lovers do. Very cutesy couple-core.'

She gives me a look so flat it could iron a shirt, but inches a little closer. I take the spoon and scoop a bite, making a show of it. My hand is controlled. My thoughts aren't.

'Open up,' I say.

'Don't you dare—'

But I already am daring, spoon held out like a challenge.

And she…leans in.

Every nerve in my body is tuned to the moment she parts her lips. I don't mean to stare. I *honestly* don't. But her bottom lip cushions the spoon – full and shaped like a problem I'd fucking love to have – then the top seals over it. She closes her eyes and draws back slowly until it's clean.

And I swear the entire restaurant blurs around her.

Holy shit.

I rock forward in my seat, refusing to picture what I'm already halfway hard for. I could devour this whole bloody dessert, and it'd do fuck all for the throb firing south every time she moves her cherry-painted, fuckable lips. This wasn't for the camera. This was real.

And if I didn't know it better, I'd think this was for me.

But that's impossible. This is Theo. List girl. Little Miss Professional. This wasn't in her brief.

Neither was my semi, come to think of it.

'Good?' Meaningless question, but I need to say something.

'Shockingly good.' She wipes the corner of her mouth with her thumb and licks it off.

My brain doesn't recover, it barely holds together as I try not to imagine what else I could feed her slowly and—

She takes the spoon from my hand and dips it into the cream.

'Your turn.' She holds it up as if it's nothing, but her cheeks give her away. Doesn't matter how calm her voice is. Her skin's telling the truth. It's adorable.

I close the distance, tongue darting out to catch the tip.

Rucked Up Ruse

Then I give it a few lazy sweeps through the cream. Am I laying it on thick? Sure. But she started it.

Theo's eyes don't waver, but her pupils dilate and the breath she draws trembles at the edges. The line between us moves in the half-second her lashes lower. In the sudden knowledge that if I wanted to kiss her right now, I wouldn't have to fake a damn thing.

That's insane. We're not dating. This is fake. Fuck's sake, it's fake. Not to speak of the fact she probably thinks I'm an arse with serious impulse control issues. And she'd be a hundred per cent right.

It's supposed to be a fake date, not foreplay.

Theo sets the spoon down. 'Photos done.'

'Aye.' My voice's gone husky.

She dabs her lower lip with her napkin, nodding.

I need a distraction, so I ask, 'What are you doing after?'

'Nothing even remotely exciting. Probably a bit of *Great British Bake Off* and that's it.'

'Slippery slope. I've heard sponge cake's a gateway drug.'

She laughs, and it lands deep, hot, and far too fucking welcome.

I cock my head, and let the smile go full tilt. 'You're too young and beautiful to spend Saturday nights alone on the couch.'

She arches a brow, her mouth curving just a little. 'Firstly, save the sweet talk. Secondly, I'm not alone.'

For a second, searing rage spears through me, and I hate whoever gets to sit beside her. Some faceless prick in chinos. Probably scrolls through his phone while she talks. 'Hope he appreciates you sharing your cake show.'

'He mostly sleeps through it.'

I sit back, keep the grin where it is. What kind of impotent, boring twat sleeps on a couch next to a stunner like Theo?

'Elvis. My cat,' she says. 'Prefers canned tuna to Victoria sponge.'

Relief flares and I chuckle.

In about half an hour, after this pretend dinner date, I'll drop her off outside her flat in Leith. Then it's back to Duncraig. Video game on, shouting at teenagers. Maybe a wank. Definitely a wank. And bed.

I turned twenty-four last month. My Saturday nights weren't meant to fizzle out before the bingo crowd went home. A few weeks ago, I'd have been out. Found someone and kept the night going until the moans drowned everything else out for a bit.

Can't do that under this spotlight. Now there are cameras and people sniffing for scandal. And sure, that's part of it. But the real kicker?

I don't want to.

I could pull. Easily. All it'd take is one look, one line. But the thought makes my skin go tight. Feels wrong in a way that I don't bother unpacking.

Doesn't mean I want to sit on that lumpy-arse couch either, controller in hand, stewing over the things I should've said to a man who's six feet under and should've heard them. Even if I spent years convincing myself he didn't deserve to.

I glance at Theo. Still perched there like she belongs in a still life. Dark hair neat, shoulders square, no clue how much I want to ask her to stay.

So I aim for casual. 'There's a small party here in Edinburgh. Low-key, the sister of a teammate turning thirty. You should come.'

She barely looks at me. 'No, thanks.'

I flash a grin. 'Fair. You and your cat got big plans. Tuna and telly, living the dream.'

Still nothing.

I wait. Then I push, because apparently I'm not done humiliating myself. 'Might be good for optics. Public-ish. Bit of strategic hand-holding. You know. For the cameras.'

She side-eyes me. 'Did you rehearse that?'

'Naw. I always improvise my charm.'

Another pause. Then she sighs, and I beam, because that sound means she's coming with me.

'Will there be group sex, Finn?'

'Probably not. But no promises,' I say, half in love with the way she tries not to smile.

Dammit. I enjoy hanging out with Theo more than I enjoy hanging out with anyone else. Too bad I'm wired wrong for good things like this.

Chapter 7

Theo

I've never seen someone high-five with their entire body before.

As soon as Finn and I step from the cobbled back lane into the converted mews – once a carriage house, now all exposed beams, stone walls, and bespoke lighting – he bounces around like a pinball, from one rugby player to another. Chest bumps, complicated handshakes, bear hugs that lift grown men off their feet.

I hover just behind him in the hallway, coat still in hand, posture snapped to attention. The floor's littered with heaps of trainers, boots, and heels. No one bothered to tidy up after themselves. I take off my Mary Janes and position them next to the umbrella holder. On second glance I realise that it's a real elephant foot.

Disgusting.

Before I can figure out where to go or what to do with my arms, a woman with perfect blonde balayage appears, Prosecco bottle in hand.

'Hi, I'm Polly! Nevin's sister?' she says when she sees my puzzled expression. 'The birthday girl. Come in properly!'

'Oh, hi. I'm Theo. And happy birthday.' I force a smile.

Rucked Up Ruse

'Sorry for showing up uninvited and without a gift. That's a bit rude. But it was also a bit spontaneous.'

She waves it away. 'Any girlfriend of Finn's is family. Though we're all shocked he's settling down.' She wiggles her eyebrows.

'Well, I—'

'Lennox, ya wee chancer!' A voice booms from what looks like the kitchen. 'Get yer daft arse in here!'

'One sec!' Finn calls back. He lights up every time someone shouts his name. I, in contrast, generally shrink a little every time someone says mine.

He turns to me and leans in. 'I'll say hi and be right back. Everyone's sound, promise. You'll be fine.'

'I know how to handle myself at parties, Lennox. The question is: do you?'

He laughs and weaves through the crowd.

Sure, I'm fine.

Just like I was fine at that client party in Shoreditch, when I stood next to the bar for an hour while Gil regurgitated *my* strategy and ideas to the room as if he'd written all of it in his sleep. No one even looked at me, because they naturally assumed it could only have emerged from his extraordinary brain. And that's when it clicked. The only person who'd ever called me brilliant – my *boyfriend* – had been using my work to elevate his standing all this time. When I tried to call him out, he told me not to make a scene. Said I was imagining things.

And just like I was fine two weeks later, when the company let me go and the girl from Nectar's HR whispered, *'you'll land on your feet'* and handed me a card signed by people who'd never once asked me to lunch.

They didn't let Gil go.

They let *me* go.

So, yeah, that was the last party I went to until now.

Since moving back to Edinburgh last spring, I haven't

been out. There's no point. I don't drink, and small talk with strangers drains me.

I have friends. Of course I do. A book club that turned into a WhatsApp group that turned into three of us sending each other cat memes. Occasional brunches and Pilates when I remember to go.

So yeah. Mostly I work. It's my happy place and my safe space. And that's the thing about control. You hold on to it with both hands. Because once you let it slip…

Finn comes out of the kitchen, heading back to me.

'Hey.' He curves his hand around my waist. Low, easy, boyfriend-casual.

His touch hits a switch that halts the rest of me. It's the familiarity that gets me, the way his fingers rest like they know where they belong.

They categorically don't.

'Want a drink, *babe*?' he asks with a wink.

His hand stays on my waist, and I don't move. 'Sure.'

A massive man with red hair in a Celtic shirt lumbers toward us, a sentient brick wall. 'Mate! Thought you'd ghosted us.'

'Was thinking about it.' Finn clasps his hand. 'Scottie, meet Theo. Theo, this is my flatmate and teammate and general pain in everyone's arse.'

Scottie's eyebrows climb. 'The girlfriend? So you're real.'

'Last I checked,' I say, too brightly.

'Right!' Finn grins. 'Drink for Theo, coming right up.'

And he disappears again, leaving me with my coat and Scottie plus a sudden urge to disappear.

'So,' Scottie sizes me up. 'What's your angle?'

'Excuse me?'

'With Finn. See, he doesn't *do* relationships.'

'People can change.'

'Sure, in general. But not so sure about him.' Scottie takes

Rucked Up Ruse

a swig of beer. 'He's my best mate, but he's a knobhead and a notorious flight risk. Always has been, as far as I can tell.'

'Maybe he needed the right reason to stay.' The words taste false on my tongue.

This is all pretend. But the edge in Scottie's scepticism makes me want to prove him wrong, even if I'm lying through my teeth.

Finn returns with a glass of Fanta, grinning as if he's performed a magic trick.

Scottie mutters something about pool, and slinks off like a sulking bear.

'See? I remembered,' Finn says proudly and hands me the glass.

Our fingers graze and there's a tiny, involuntary tug low in my stomach.

'Impressive. Most men can't recall what I said five minutes ago.'

'I'm not most men.' He closes the gap, his body aligned with mine, as he steers us forward deeper into the party.

Built behind the Georgian townhouses, these mews are tucked all through Edinburgh's New Town. Today, they're worth millions. This one is quite big and packed with rugby players, their partners, friends, and other guests. About forty, fifty people? Most of them are watching us with varying degrees of subtlety. Finn's palm stays where it is. Not possessive, but present.

My ribcage tightens, stupidly aware of the contact. 'Everyone's staring at you, Finn.'

'They're staring at *you*,' he counters. 'Can't blame them. You're a sight to behold.'

'Okay, so they're staring at us then. Happy?'

'More than I've been in a while.'

A blonde in a glittery top glances over, her gaze lingering on Finn before sliding to me with naked curiosity.

'Three o'clock. Sequins. She's wondering what kind of spell I used on you to make you behave and follow me,' I say.

'And what's your professional assessment?' He presses the heel of his hand lightly into my back. The contact writes itself across my spine. I try not to read it.

'That she should wonder what kind of spell I'll use on her if she doesn't stop gawking.'

He laughs. 'There's the clawed kitty. I was starting to worry you'd gone soft.'

'Never.' I sip my drink. 'Though your teammates seem convinced I'm either a saint or a scam.'

'Which would you prefer?'

'Neither. I'm just doing my job. Overtime, by the way.'

His smile dims slightly. 'Right.'

Someone calls his name, and he introduces me to a blur of faces. Nevin, the birthday girl's brother. His shy girlfriend Ava. Two other players whose names I immediately forget. Polly's doctor friends. They're all watching us like we're a new Netflix series they're not sure about yet.

Finn drapes his heavy, muscular arm around my shoulders while spinning a training story. His arm stays there, thumb brushing slow arcs over the curve of my upper arm, so casually I almost don't notice.

Almost.

In truth, my body records each touch, time-stamping the moment. His hand on my back at 9:17. His fingers brushing mine at 9:24. His arm around me at 9:38.

'Selfie time!' Polly appears with her phone. 'Everyone squeeze in!'

Finn pulls me closer. Just before the flash, he presses his lips to my cheek. Warm. Soft. Lingering.

He doesn't let go after the photo. His mouth stays close to my ear. 'You okay?'

I nod, not trusting my voice.

Rucked Up Ruse

Across the room, two women whisper, glancing our way. I catch fragments: '...porn pictures...' and '...shag sandwich...'

Of course they're talking about it. Everyone is.

'Ignore them,' Finn says quietly. 'If I can do it, you can do it.'

But that glint behind his eyes sharpens, too fast for anyone else to catch. I see it. The micro-shift in his posture, tension notched at the corners of his mouth. He's playing the charming rogue they expect, but something underneath is crumbling.

'I'm fine.' There, I said it again.

'You're not.' His eyes hold mine. 'But thanks for pretending.'

'Says the expert. But isn't that why we're here?'

His brows pull in, just barely. 'Some parts more than others.'

Before I have the chance to ask what he means, Scottie reappears. 'Lennox, we're playing pool. You in?'

'Naw, staying with my girl.'

'I can entertain myself,' I say. 'Go play, *babe*.'

'You sure?'

'Positive. I'll watch you lose from here.'

His grin returns full force. 'Cheeky.'

As he walks away into the billiard room – because that's the kind of house we're in – I catch myself watching him. The easy confidence in his shoulders. The way people orbit around him naturally. On paper, he shouldn't fit here. Edinburgh's full of polished vowels and private school grins, people who know which fork to use and which intern's uncle runs a hedge fund. But Finn Lennox doesn't shrink to fit, he carves his space. Not with pedigree, with presence and charm that doesn't beg to be liked, only dares you not to. And somehow, they all respond. Men lean in, women laugh too loudly, no one asks where he went to school.

'Enjoying the view?' Polly edges in beside me, glass in

hand, smile playing at the corner of her mouth. 'He's different with you.'

'We haven't been together long. It's only just getting serious.'

'That's not what I meant.' She studies me over her glass. 'He's usually putting on a show. Big gestures, big laughs, silly jokes all the time. Class clown vibes. With you, he's...watching. Checking in. It's sweet.'

I give her the kind of smile that works better in mirrors. 'Oh, he's full of surprises.'

'I bet. Though I'm surprised you're cool with...you know. The video and all that.'

'We're working through it.' The lie is as smooth as sea-glass.

'Of course. And I don't want to pry but that must have been hard. Seeing him with...two other women...like that.' The sympathy in her voice doesn't reach her eyes. They're a touch too glossy and curious. As if she's halfway to picturing the whole thing in 4K. She's not comforting me, she's grazing, testing for soft tissue. Looking for gossip, for the tender spot to sink her teeth into.

Luckily, there is none. But I have to fake it, so I let my eyes flutter and lower my head. 'It was. It is. But some things are worth the effort.'

'You're so strong. I hope it all goes well.' She pats my arm, and I wish she wouldn't. Realising that I'm not spilling the beans, she swans off to the next group of people.

Hope it all goes well? The fuck you do, Polly.

I drift toward the pool table where Finn's lining up his shot. The cue glides through his fingers. A lanky guy with bloodshot eyes sways beside him, beer sloshing over his knuckles.

'I'm curious, mate. How did it work?' he slurs. 'One on your cock, one on your face? Or did they both fight to gag first?'

Rucked Up Ruse

My blood crystallises. 'Apologise,' I say with the calm of a glacier.

'C'mon. It's a joke, princess. Lighten—'

'It wasn't funny the first time your lizard brain squeezed it out.' I take a slow step forward. 'Try again, *mate*.'

Finn straightens, surprise flickering across his face.

'Chill, *Bella*,' the guy mutters, suddenly interested in his beer.

Finn sets his palm to my shoulder, quiet and sure, and most of the adrenaline settles. 'Didn't know you played defence, darlin'.'

'Neither did I.' Our eyes lock. 'Temporary position.'

Okay. I didn't want to do it, but I guess it's time to assert some dominance. So I vent a breath, hand him my drink, and step into the light.

'Rack 'em,' I say.

Scottie blinks. 'You play?'

'Only when someone deserves to lose.'

The lanky guy opens his mouth. I shut it with a head-mistress-level stern look. Another of my specialities.

Scottie grins like this is the best part of his night. 'Right then. What's the wager?'

'Fifty.' I chalk a cue. 'But if you're skint, we can play for pride.' I nod towards the lanky guy leaning against the table. 'C'mon, big man. Let's play. Just you and me.'

He scoffs. 'What, so you can cry when you lose?'

'No. So I can make you wish you'd kept your mouth shut.'

He shifts, about to answer—

'Naw,' Scottie cuts in, stepping between us. 'She plays me.'

I narrow one eye. 'Is that so?'

'Better game.' He tosses me a cue. 'Less mess, trust me.'

Scottie racks them with care, chalks his cue, sizing me up. I shrug and break. Two stripes drop in quick succession, corner and side. A clean split. The table opens up as if it's on my side.

A low whistle from someone behind me. Scottie just nods.

'Stripes,' I say, cool and unbothered, and circle the table.

Next shot, clean. Third – banked off the cushion and in. I line up again. My grip's sure and my tempo's slow. In the end, it's all muscle memory. Four, five, six – gone.

The room's quieter now. Even Finn's still.

I glance up, just once, meet Scottie's eyes. 'You keeping count?'

His beer stills halfway to his mouth, and he doesn't answer.

Seven sinks with the softest kiss of felt. I straighten, and take my time chalking up for the black.

'You're letting me win, right?' I say.

Scottie huffs. 'Sure.'

I line it up. Gentle angle, centre pocket. My stance is solid and deliberate. No theatrics, I don't need them. Cue slides. Tap. The eight ball rolls, slow and perfect, and drops like it's been waiting for me all night.

Silence.

Then Finn, quietly behind me: 'Fucking hell.'

I take my glass from his hands and a long sip from my juice, then rest the cue on the edge of the table. 'That's me warmed up. Who's next?'

Someone mutters, 'Hell no. Fuck that.'

'Think we're good,' Scottie says, hands raised like I'm armed. 'I, erm…value my ego.'

I flash him a tight smile. 'Wise.'

But I'm not done, I want more. Another game. The buzz is electric and hot under my skin, and I haven't felt this alive in over a year. There even was a time I'd have killed to go pro. But Dad had other plans, so that was that.

That's when Finn sidles up beside me, close enough to count his breaths. 'Didn't know you had that in you.'

'There wasn't much else to do in Elie. Pub or church. And I'm not a spiritual person.'

Rucked Up Ruse

Finn dips in close, low voice brushing the shell of my ear. 'Awright, pool shark. Time to channel that murder energy somewhere safer.'

I don't move. 'Like where?'

His smile comes cocked, loaded, and aimed at me. 'Dance floor. Come on, before you start biting throats.'

My pulse still ricochets in my palms as Finn threads our fingers and steers me away. And I follow. Still charged and sparking, but I let him lead.

The dining room is dim, the table shoved to the side to make room, and full of people swaying to whatever remix is thumping from the Bluetooth speaker. Someone's switched on fairy lights. Someone else spilled rum on the fishbone parquet. No one cares.

Finn faces me, one hand already on my waist.

'Do you even dance?' I squint up at him.

'Darlin'…' He eases closer. 'I'm a flanker. I move my body in unexpected ways and have very flexible hips. It's what I do for a living.'

I tip my head back, exasperated, but it's useless. I'm already moving with him, body still humming from the pool kill. And he keeps grinning, as though he's suspected it all along and had been waiting to see this version of me.

'Better now? Got that out of your system, then?' he asks.

'Don't push it. Pool is my favourite game,' I say. But I'm smiling.

My hands find uncertain ground. One on his shoulder, the other grazing his side. The bass is low and slow. Remixed nineties R&B, sticky with suggestion. It swells and coils around the room. People move to the syrupy rhythm, hips rocking, bodies pressed too close. It's roasting in here.

Finn doesn't say anything. He just steps into me until we're flush, the press of his chest against my dress a question he's not ready to ask out loud. He smells like rumpled sheets, skin-warm citrus, and whatever alchemy turns boy into man, cocky into risky.

And then we move.

Not dancing, it's more swaying. Gravity pulling us together molecule by molecule. He settles his hand lower, right at that boundary between safe and suggestive. My blood fizzes under his touch, and I don't know if it's the music or the temperature, but his inhale stalls halfway when I look up.

We're not speaking, but something's definitely happening. And I'm powerless to stop it.

I tighten my fingers on his shirt and catch the shadow of his jaw as he watches me. His forehead tips toward mine, close enough that I feel the heat of it before our skin meets. I'm not breathing right. Not blinking either. My body's holding still so I don't break the spell.

His nose brushes mine. Our mouths don't touch, but they hover. And that spot – right at the curve between his nostril and his lip – floods me. A pure hit of him, dark and delicious. It lands at the back of my tongue and melts there. I could drink it. I could drown. He exhales, lips parting like he's about to say something, but then…doesn't. Instead, he leans in a fraction closer. My pulse skitters, and my whole body's straining forward.

One more millimetre and we'd fall over the edge.

He pulls me in, slow but sure. The line disappears. We're right there. The music fades, the heat dims, and there's nothing but him. If he kisses me now, I won't stop it.

I *want* him to.

I want to taste what he's not saying. This – whatever this is turning into – isn't all pretend anymore. There's something else underneath, some form of kinship or recognition.

That's the moment I know I'm in fucking trouble.

My brain slams the brakes and screams in warning. The room keeps pulsing around us. I can't… I'm not ready. This was supposed to be a job, a favour, a performance. Not *this*.

Rucked Up Ruse

Not...*him*.

Because I don't do this. This isn't safe. This isn't smart.

This is how I *fall*.

And when I do, I won't get up again.

So I step back like I've been burned. My hands drop and my body retreats before my brain can catch up.

'I-I...erm...need some air.'

And then I turn without looking at him or waiting for a reply. Just out, out, out. Away from the music, the heat, the eyes. Finn. I shoulder past the girl in sequins and apologise without stopping. The music fuzzes out as I hit the hallway, the air cooler and sharper, but still too thick.

Not enough. I need to leave. Now. I slip into my shoes.

I'm stupid. So stupid.

Outside, the night smacks me across the face with January chill. Edinburgh, smug and indifferent. I keep walking down the cobbled lane towards the street. Head down. My block heels catch once on the uneven stones, but I don't slow down. I gulp air like I'm surfacing from a riptide I should never have let pull me under.

Fuck.

That was the edge of a cliff. And I nearly jumped. Voluntarily.

'Theo.' His voice knifes through the hush. Not loud, but urgent enough to make me stop.

Still, I don't turn.

Footsteps close the gap. I mean, he runs for a living, so what was I thinking? Of course he'd eat up the distance between us in no time. Then he's beside me, breath visible in the streetlight.

'You forgot your coat,' he says, holding it up.

'No, I didn't.' I take it anyway and pull it on.

'I see.' He keeps his eyes on me. 'You awright, love?'

I huff a laugh. It sounds nothing like one. 'Do you think I'm all right?'

'Think you're wee bit shook from the…dance.'

'No shit, Sherlock.'

'We should go back in,' he says eventually. 'They might talk.'

'Let them.'

He cocks his head. 'That's not what you want.'

'I don't know what I want.' And this is true on so many levels.

'Come back in, Theo. Just for a bit.'

For a second, I actually consider it. His voice is too soft, his face too open, and there's heat still clinging to my skin from everything we didn't do. I want to say yes. Or I want to want to. But I can't.

He waits. Long enough for it to sting. Then he nods. 'Okay. Then let's get you a taxi.'

I let him walk me to the kerb, this man I'm fake-dating and real-wanting, who makes me feel seen in ways I didn't agree to.

As the car pulls up minutes later, I know one thing for sure: I can't fall to bits over a single hit of his potent pheromones. Not when both our careers are on the line.

If I let myself fall for him, it won't be pretend. It'll be real.

And it'll hurt.

Chapter 8

Finn

Back at the party, the vibe's gone staler than day-old crisps. I fish an Irn Bru out of the fridge and crack it open, letting the fizz hit my tongue. Bodies slump on sofas, and someone's out cold in a party hat. Polly's shouting about going to a club, her makeup smudged beneath one eye. Next to her, a man who has anaesthetist vibes is doing bumps of ket off his phone.

I've never understood why people think athletes are the unhinged ones. If they want to see people getting off their absolute fucking tits, go spend a night with doctors. They're the worst. Probably because they shake hands with death every day.

'Lennox! You coming?' Scottie appears, keys jangling.

'You've been drinking. Who's driving?'

'Mikey's girl. Or I can drive back to Duncraig with you later? Polly said we're off to The Drum Vault.'

'Naw, mate.' I take another swig. I'd rather pry off my toe nails one by one than dance to house remixes with a fake smile on my face tonight. 'Head's wrecked.'

'We don't have a game tomorrow, ya boring wee shite.' His gaze tightens with suspicion. 'Where's the pool menace?'

'She went home.'

'Did you scare her off already?'

I run my tongue along my front teeth. 'Shut up, Kerr.'

'Awright. I like her.' Scottie's swaying slightly. 'But that pool game? Damn, the state of that.'

I let out a low sound through my nose. That memory's already got me fucked. How Theo decimated Scottie without breaking a sweat. Those blue eyes focussed, that little smile when she sank the black. Confident, deadly, and magnetic. That wasn't the polite, buttoned-up planner who triple-checks the calendar and dodges compliments like they're knives.

No, that was the version who fucks you up and walks away whistling.

And Jesus Christ, I wanted to follow.

Couldn't stop staring at that arse – high and round, bent over. All I could think about was stepping in behind her. Hand on her hip, mouth at her neck. Tugging those tights down nice and slow while she lined up the shot like nothing was happening. Letting her sink the black with me balls-deep and biting back a groan. And—

'Weird though.' Scottie interrupts me, and I'm glad.

I'm too old to run around parties with a hard-on.

'What?' I shoot back, a bit too harshly.

'You, Lennox. Actually caring.'

'I care about loads of things.'

'Rugby. Gym. Video games. Your silly hair.' He counts on his fingers. 'Never women as far as I can tell. I mean, not in that way.'

I drain half the can. The sugar coats my teeth, but the drink does nothing to budge the weight behind my sternum. As if I've swallowed a bag of cement.

Theo.

Fucking hell.

I almost kissed her.

Those fucking lips.

Rucked Up Ruse

They were right there. Her breath brushed my chin, body pressed to mine, tits crushed to my chest, soft and real and fucking lethal. She wanted it, and I knew she'd let me.

But then she jerked back as if I'd burned her and left me standing in the middle of that room with my heart pounding, my cock hard, and every last nerve tuned to her like she was still touching me.

'Earth to Lennox!'

I blink. 'What?'

'I said we're going to the club now. Last chance.'

'Hard pass. But have fun, ya prick.' I give Scottie a whack on his back.

After they leave, I slump onto the couch, phone in hand. My thumb hovers over Theo's name. I want to text her, but what would I even say?

Sorry I nearly kissed you for real when we're supposed to be faking it?

The screen goes dark, and I toss it aside. This is getting far too complicated, and she's not interested. She's polite, professional, and probably plotting my murder in her sleep for messing with her. I keep telling myself the ache in my gut is the sugar from the Irn Bru, and that I didn't want to follow her home and ask what the hell just happened.

Instead, I do what any emotionally stunted man does when things get too real: fuck all.

Time to get all that liquid out of my system. I squeeze past strangers in the narrow hallway, mumbling 'sorry' and 'shift yer arse please' until I reach the toilet door. It's locked.

'Finn Lennox. Thought you'd bolted.'

The blonde girl in the sequins. What's her name? Tara? Tina? A T-name that isn't Theo. She staggers toward me, glass empty but smile full. Sequins catch the dim light, winking as if she's in on some joke I haven't heard.

'Just waiting for the loo,' I say, nodding towards the door.

'I saw your girlfriend leave.' She inches closer.

Her perfume hits me first, some decadent stuff. I don't care. I want to smell Theo.

'You two beefing?' she asks.

'Nope.'

Her hand lands on my chest. 'Don't tell me you're *actually* dating her.'

The wall bumps against my shoulders as I step back. 'We are, aye.'

She laughs. 'Doesn't look like the type who'd let you blow off steam the way you need to.'

Her body leans into mine like she's already made the decision for both of us. Not a single mixed signal. Only sex on a plate, ready to snack.

'You're way too hot to be pretending not to want this.' Her fingers trail down my stomach, hovering at my belt.

Six months ago, I'd have her jeans around her ankles in the cupboard by now. Even last month, I might've flirted back.

But tonight?

All I can think about is Theo's face when she left. The panic in her eyes. How fast she pulled away.

I can't fuck this up.

To my surprise, my dick agrees. Couldn't be less interested as Sequin Girl leans in.

'Don't,' I say, my hand firm on her shoulder. 'Already taken.'

'Are you *serious*?' Her eyes widen. 'I've seen you handle two at once, so…'

'Stop it.'

She takes a step back, her face is twisted between offence and confusion. 'Your loss.'

The bathroom door opens and some bloke stumbles out. I slip past him and lock the door behind me. Silence floods the room and presses in. I turn on the tap, full blast. Let it roar, just so I don't have to hear the thoughts racing around in my skull. I stare at myself in the mirror. Same face. Same front. Same broken bits stitched behind the eyes.

Theo walked away. And that blonde? Didn't care, just wanted a show. Neither of them meant to gut me. But it lands like they did.

It starts in my chest. A slow, sick compression. The water keeps running, but there's not enough sound to cover what's clawing its way up. I grip the sink. Palms clammy, neck damp, pulse kicking like it's trying to escape my throat. This used to happen when I was a boy. After the shouting, not during. Afterwards, when my mum didn't speak to me, didn't look at me. When it was over. When it was supposed to be fine.

Don't fucking fall apart. Not here. Not now.

I blink hard. But the heat stays. Pressed behind my eyes, thick and burning. Bit by bit, the world pulls back as if someone hit mute. The room narrows. I swear I smell mildew and second-hand smoke. Back to sixteen. Bin bag in one hand, the other braced against the door my maw had just slammed.

That time, she meant it. 'You're a waste of space, Finn. Piss off. And don't come back.'

My body tenses for impact, even when nothing touches me. Everything feels temporary. If I move wrong, the world will teeter, crumble, and I'll be locked out again. My body registers the old gut-deep, stomach-sick panic. That cold rush down my back, my chest clamping shut.

I bite the inside of my cheek until I taste metal and grip the sink harder, trying to focus on the cold porcelain. On the sound of the water. I squeeze my eyes shut and wait. Let the wave pass. Let it claw at my ribs, but not pull me under.

Ten.

Nine.

Eight.

By five, the background noise starts to return. By two, my heart's still hammering, but at least it's not trying to punch through my ribcage anymore. I open my eyes. The lad in the mirror looks like me but drained and shaken. I splash water on my face, but it doesn't help.

Fuck.

This is why I don't do feelings. Why I don't date. Why I keep it light and filthy and forgettable. Because when it starts meaning something, it stops being safe. I felt it tonight. Her hand in mine, her eyes locked on my mouth. But nobody fucking stays. Not when you're too loud and too much and too fucked up. Not when they catch a glimpse of the real you and realise there's no fixing it.

Theo doesn't know what I am. Doesn't know about the kid who learned to perform to get fed and not beaten up, who got good at jokes so he didn't get a thrashing. Who clawed his way out of a piss-stained stairwell and decided that if he wasn't wanted, he could at least be watched.

She doesn't see what's under the charm yet. And I hope she never does.

I know what it costs to carry someone else's damage. And Theo's already carrying enough. She's bending over backwards to make this work. To keep her job and save Charlie's agency. To protect me from every whisper and fake headline and sleazy bawbag at a party who thinks he can say whatever he wants.

There's no way I'm dragging her down with me.

Even if part of me wants to close the space between us anyway, counting down to the next time I get to touch her.

Chapter 9

Theo

Rain comes at me sideways. Stirling's weather forecast promised 'light precipitation', which is meteorologist-speak for 'prepare to drown standing up'. My fringe's sticking to my forehead like seaweed, and my wool coat now weighs seventeen stone.

But the cameras are rolling, so I smile.

Scrubby grass flattens under the wind, the Ochils crouch in the distance, dull green under a sky that can't decide between grey and greyer. Trees lean in the wind, bare-limbed and stubborn.

The Rebels' new stadium reeks of wet grass and fried food. Lads in puffer jackets crowd under umbrellas, shouting over each other about tactics like they're on the coaching staff. The stands pulse with anticipation, half-empty but twice as loud as they should be. What the local rugby fans might lack in numbers, they make up for in volume and creative profanity.

Charlie texts:

All set? 💋

. . .

I smile and type back:

> All ready. Position secured. Kiss arranged. Operation Dummy Pass ✅

My stomach flips at the word 'kiss'. It sounds harmless enough for what I've orchestrated. A performance piece and strategic photo opportunity. Nothing more than optics.

But after that moment at the party …

Finn emerges from the tunnel with the team. He's transformed in his kit. Pink hair slicked back by rain, shorts hugging his thighs in ways that would probably get flagged on TikTok. He moves like the rules are optional and every eye belongs on him.

'Look who it is.' His voice cuts through the din as he jogs toward me. 'My good luck charm.'

'Save it for the cameras.' I click my nail against my watch. 'Two minutes till kick-off. Quick peck on the cheek, then you're off.'

'Of course, darlin'.' He shoots me that crooked smile.

'Let's not make this harder than your thighs,' I say.

Finn smirks with the cheeky arrogance of a man who's going to reply with something I'll regret hearing. 'My thighs are not the har—'

'I swear, if you finish that sentence, I—'

The cameras swing our way. Perfect timing. I rise on tiptoes, aiming for his cheek as planned. Sweet, supportive girlfriend appropriate.

But Finn turns an inch at the last second. His lips brush the corner of my mouth. Not quite a kiss, but more than we

Rucked Up Ruse

agreed. Heat rushes through me, pooling right where I shouldn't feel anything. My cheeks blaze so fast I half-expect steam to rise.

This isn't part of the job. This isn't part of the job. This isn't part of the damn job.

He pulls back, eyes locked on mine. 'For luck.'

My pulse jack-knifes and he fucking knows it. I speak through a shield of fingers, just in case anyone's trying to read my lips. 'We agreed it'd be the cheek.'

Finn reins in a wolfish smile and lifts his hand, too. 'I changed tactics.'

'Without consulting me.'

'Would you have said yes?' His question hangs between us.

'Irrelevant.' My voice splinters. 'This isn't real, Finn.'

'Oh, I know.' He wipes water off my cheek with his knuckle. 'Now watch me get us a real win.'

Then he's jogging backward, still facing me, that insufferable smirk stamped onto his face. The stadium lights catch raindrops on his cheeks. I've never seen anything more magnetic in my life.

And I hate that I smile back.

I file the moment under hazards of contact sports.

Next item on the list: feigning excitement for *my boyfriend* rolling around in the mud.

My feet find the steps to the VIP box on autopilot. The air inside is sterile, smelling of new flooring and old money. Knox Montgomery, the Canadian founder and owner of the Stirling Rebels, had the five thousand seater stadium finished just about a year ago. It's the first home fixture of the new year, after last week's away opener. I wish Charlie were here. She's missing the match because she's at a charity gala in the Highlands, schmoozing potential clients we've been chasing for months. Black tie, big cash. One more step to Elite Edge's survival.

The whistle shrills, a sharp, clean sound that slices through my thoughts. The game explodes into motion.

I find my designated seat, a plastic throne of corporate hospitality, and sink into it. My coat drips onto the floor and my notebook's already warping, ink bleeding through bullet points. *Operational focus* underlined twice. *Client boundaries* circled so hard the paper nearly tears. I have to concentrate.

Instead, I'm remembering his breath against mine at the party a week ago. The weight of his hand on my waist. How he looked at me when I ran, as if I'd pocketed something vital.

I pull up the restaurant photos from our dinner date that night on my phone for the gazillionth time. Even I can't tell myself that I'm that obsessed with them only for professional reasons.

It's just... The photographer captured a story we never told.

There's one image of Finn watching me, my head thrown back in a laugh I don't remember letting loose. His expression isn't for the cameras; it's quiet and focussed, trying to memorise my joy. My thumb hovers over the image of his gaze. Gil never saw me like that. After the initial charm offensive – or love-bombing – wore off, his eyes would skim over me, assessing and calculating. His touch was a transaction, his praise a down payment on my next brilliant idea he could claim as his. He took my light and used it to illuminate himself, leaving me in the shadows he'd created. Gil made me shrink, sucking the life out of me with one narcissistic move after the next.

Finn makes me feel visible. And after Gil, that's its own kind of fear.

I press the heel of my palm to my brow, pulling myself out of it. This is good, I tell myself. The story is selling – the pink-haired rogue and the PR girl who tamed him. It's a narrative people can digest and savour.

Rucked Up Ruse

The near-kiss was a blip. The moment on the pitch was a calculated risk. Even though that cheeky kiss still burns.

Anyhoo, the cameras caught it, and by tomorrow morning, those images will be everywhere. I've handled worse assignments. I've certainly handled worse men. I'm perfectly capable of containing this.

A steward offers me a Bovril. I decline with a shudder and try to make mental notes. *Monday meeting: leverage the 'good luck charm' angle. Pitch a Valentine's Day feature. Follow up with* Sports Weekly.

But my focus narrows and hooks on the number seven shirt. On the bright flare of pink hair in a scrum. Over the course of the game, I watch him move. He's made of kinetic energy and feral grace. When he has the ball, he doesn't just run; he devours the grass. He's dancing.

The small crowd erupts, and I catch the movement just in time – Finn sprinting down the pitch, ball tucked against his side, a defender closing in fast. My heart vaults into my throat as the larger man slams into him, driving him into the muck.

'Get up, Lennox,' I mutter, not realising I've spoken aloud until the woman beside me chuckles.

'First rugby match?'

'No.' I smooth my hair. 'Just the first one where I care if someone breaks their neck.'

She nods knowingly. 'My husband plays. I still close my eyes during tackles.'

Finn bounces to his feet, shaking off the hit as if it's nothing. He pats Brodie's back, grinning through the mud and rain. When he glances toward the stands, I swear he finds me instantly, like there's some invisible thread connecting us.

He gives me a thumbs up. He knows I'm worried. And my skin goes hot, neck to knees.

The rain intensifies and turns the pitch into a quagmire. Players skid and crash. Finn collides with a prop twice his width, wiggling out of the hold with a raw power that makes the crowd scream.

When he scores, the stadium erupts, and he points directly at me before being mobbed by teammates.

'Lennox is brilliant today,' the woman next to me says.

I suppose he is. Every move sharp, every decision precise. My phone pings with notifications. Social media's already on fire with the gesture.

Not him pointing after the try 😭😭😭
I hope she doesn't regret taking him back.
Forget the try, that look he gave her should be illegal.
Finn pls. We saw that. 🔥
Concentrate on the game, pal!!

I should be pleased. This is precisely what we planned. Sure, the ghost of his scandal still haunts the algorithm. But all in all, engagement's up and negativity's down. The strategy remains sound.

And I remain entirely unmoved by the way his kit clings to his thighs and chest and—

Then it happens.

The final minutes of the first half bleed away. Finn gets the ball near the halfway line, weaving through a wall of opposition players. He's a blur of pink and blue, a force of nature. He's almost clear when a tank of a player comes at him from the side. The tackle isn't illegal, I think, but brutal.

Finn goes down. This time, he doesn't get up.

The air in my lungs turns to glass. My notebook drops from my grasp, scattering pages across the damp floor. A collective hush ripples through the stands, even the rain seems to pause.

Rucked Up Ruse

Ten seconds. Twenty. Thirty. Medics are sprinting onto the pitch.

My body moves before my brain can issue a single, rational command. I'm on my feet, shoving past the corporate suits. My heels clatter a hectic rhythm on the concrete steps.

'Miss MacMickin!' One of the match day liaisons calls from the doorway.

I ignore him, and protocol goes up in flames. I'm already halfway there. I barrel into the restricted corridor at a near run, my sodden coat flapping behind me. A security guard with a neck like a tree trunk steps into my path, arm outstretched.

'Staff only, miss.'

'I'm his emergency contact.' The lie comes out absolute. I brandish my all-access pass, my face set in a mask of authority I don't feel. 'Now move, please.'

He hesitates, caught off guard by my tone. It's enough. I move past him, pushing through a set of double doors and into the echoing concrete tunnel. The air is thick with the smell of sweat, dirt, and something metallic that ties my stomach into knots.

I find the medical bay just as they're helping Finn onto an examination table. He's shirtless, his torso a roadmap of bruises, old tattoos, and fresh scrapes. A medic is dabbing at a cut above his right eye.

There's blood.

Oh god.

But... He's fine. He's breathing. And he's pissed off.

Relief slams through me, and I wobble forward with weak knees, composure barely hanging on. My hand finds his arm without permission, my fingers digging into the muscle.

'What happened? Are you okay?'

Slowly, he turns his head in my direction. His eyes find mine, and he smiles through the blood. The medic pauses, cotton swab held aloft.

Finn grits his teeth as he adjusts. 'Dinnae worry, darlin'. Just a scratch.'

'A scratch?' My voice is tight and unfamiliar. I lean in to inspect the cut. It's clean but deep, a crimson line slashing his eyebrow. Blood runs towards his temple. 'You were down for forty-one seconds. I counted.'

A slow grin spreads across his face, pulling at the cut and making him tense. 'Didn't know you cared that much, List Girl.'

'I don't.' The denial is automatic, a reflex. 'A head injury is a complication we don't need.'

'No, we don't need that.' His gaze is intense, stripping away my pathetic excuse. He sees the tremor in my hand, still clamped to his biceps. He sees the panic I'm wrestling down. 'Complication. Is that what you call it when you look like you've seen a ghost?'

'I'm managing a potential crisis,' I insist, finally dropping my hand.

The skin where I touched him feels hot. I take a step back and lace my arms tight across my torso, trying to rebuild my fortress.

'Pure poetry,' Finn says, his voice soft now. He gestures for the medic to continue. 'Theodora MacMickin, always on the job.'

The medic cleans the wound with an antiseptic wipe. Finn sucks in a sharp breath but his eyes never leave mine. He's not looking at my professional façade, he's seeing straight through it.

'Your eyebrow is going to look like Vanilla Ice's,' I say.

'Didn't peg you for the vanilla type, MacMickin. But hey, I'm adaptable.'

I shake my head.

Unbelievable.

The medic tapes a strip of gauze over the cut. Finn winces. I should say something useful or comforting. But all I can see is blood. All I register is the phantom imprint of his skin under my hand.

I back off to give the medic more space. 'You're in good hands,' I say, voice thinner than I want. 'See you in a bit.'

'Bye, *babe*.'

I turn to leave and my legs are rubber. My coat's soaked and heavy, but it's the weight under my ribs that nearly floors me. A cold, coiled fear I thought I'd outgrown. Teenage me, hovering in doorways, listening for sounds that meant Mum was making it out of bed. That she'd eaten. That she was still…here. That panic. Same shape and weight. Same trap. I go back into the tunnel, heels echoing on wet concrete, trying to put distance between us.

I've been there before. Sick with worry and powerless anyway. Holding on to nothing but the fear they won't get back up.

And I can't do it again.

Chapter 10

Finn

'It's a scratch.' I bounce my knee, and the office chair rocks with it. 'And we lost. That's not a coincidence.'

It's been four days since the match, and I'm still raging they benched me after halftime.

Charlie leans back, steepling her fingers. She has this way of watching you that makes you shrink, a bug under her collector's pin.

'The team has a concussion protocol for a reason, Finn. You took a significant impact.'

'Aye, and I was ready to go back out. The doc was being a fanny.'

'The doctor was being a doctor.' She keeps her tone flat. 'Your long-term health is more important than one half of one game.'

'Tell that to the league table.' I slump down in the seat, and barricade my chest with my forearms. This place is all glass and brick and the faint smell of stale coffee. It's too quiet. Too clean. I need mud. I need anything other than this sterile box where my fuck-ups get dissected.

The door clicks open, and the entire atmosphere in the room shifts. Like opening the curtains to let the sun in.

Rucked Up Ruse

Of course it's her. Even the fucking air changes when she walks in.

Theo sweeps in with a stack of files in one arm and a tin of shortbread balanced on top. She's wearing a dark green dress today, one with a collar that makes her come off as tidy and untouchable. Her hair's pulled back, not a single strand out of place. The polar opposite of the rain-soaked mess from the match.

And fuck me if that didn't do something to me, knowing she gave a shit. That for one breathless minute, I wasn't just a client or colleague. I was someone worth panicking over.

'Morning.' She places the files on Charlie's desk and pops the lid on the biscuit tin. 'Brought reinforcements.'

'A woman after my own heart.' Charlie beams and takes one.

'Snack sisters,' Theo says.

'Fmack fifpeff', Charlie agrees with her mouth full.

They are sweet. And also steeled professionals with shark-like instincts. I'm lucky to have them clean up my mess.

In the glass wall, I catch the stitches bisecting my eyebrow. 'Battle scars, eh? Makes me seem brooding and mysterious.'

Theo's gaze skims over the cut for a fraction of a second before dropping to her tablet. 'It makes you seem like you've been in a fight with a stapler. Okay, so the social engagement metrics dipped by eighteen per cent.'

The numbers give her a shield to hide behind. She looks away, but not before I see it. A hint of softness, something that isn't on one of her spreadsheets. I want to poke it. I want to see what happens if I lean across this desk and trace the line of her jaw. I want to kiss that stern, clipped drawl right off her lips until she's breathless and clinging to me as she did in the med-bay four days back.

I shove the thought down, far below deck.

'The interviews.' Charlie's voice yanks me back to the room. 'What's the verdict, Theo?'

Theo swipes a finger across her tablet. Her nails are painted a glossy cherry red without any dots. 'Sentiment analysis is mixed. The *Herald* piece landed well enough. They framed it as a young talent under immense pressure.'

'See? Talented,' I chip in.

'The *Tatler* profile, however, was less favourable.' She keeps her eyes on the screen. 'They described you as an "unhinged rogue with a knack for rampant hedonism".'

'I'll take it. Sounds better than "unemployed".' I swipe a piece of shortbread from the tin.

Charlie leans forward, her pleasant expression gone. 'It sounds like a risk and bad press going to happen, Finn. Which is precisely how Knox Montgomery is starting to see you.'

'The owner?'

'Yeah, and he's not the only one. I've had word that Lord Dalcrieff is turning the screws behind the scenes.'

The biscuit sticks to the roof of my mouth. Dalcrieff. The Tory MP with a chin you could open a tin on and the fiancée I'd accidentally…entertained. 'He's just pissed off that his woman has a refined taste in men.'

'He's pissed off that you're still on the team,' Charlie corrects, her voice sharp as broken glass. 'He's been making calls. Quietly, of course. Leaning on sponsors. Reminding people how much this reflects on the club's values. And let's just say I personally don't feel charitable towards cheating engaged people, as you might know.'

Ah, right. Callum. That evil dick who cheated on Charlie with the TV presenter he's now going to marry instead of her. I know she's happy as a clam with Brodie, but that must still sting.

'What values? Winning?' I try for a laugh but it falls flat.

Theo's sharp blue gaze nails me in place. 'The value of not having your star flanker's arse and dick plastered across the internet, probably.'

The jab is clean and surgical. Right to the bone and well deserved.

Charlie releases a measured exhale that drains the room. 'We lost the Jessica Adair account this morning.'

I frown. 'The tennis player?'

'That's the one.' She drops her hand, her expression grim. 'Said she couldn't risk the "association". The point stands, Finn. I'm taking hits for you. This scandal has wiped half the goodwill we built the first half of the season. And the press won't drop it because, sadly, you look good naked.'

A searing spike of shame pierces my chest. It's one thing for me to be in the shite. It's another to take them down with me. I stare at the grain of the desk, at a tiny coffee ring near the edge. 'I'm sorry.'

'Don't be sorry,' Charlie says. 'Be useful. Loyalty isn't a renewable resource. It's a choice. And I'm choosing to stick it out with you. Don't make me regret that.'

She twists the Montblanc pen between her fingers. 'Who filmed it?'

My head snaps up. 'What?'

'The video. Who put the camera in the room?' She leans forward again. 'It wasn't a security feed.'

'It wasn't them,' I say instantly. A gut reaction. 'The sisters. Not a chance.'

Theo raises a sculpted eyebrow. 'You seem awfully certain.'

'They've got proper careers. One's a barrister, the other works in finance, according to my research.' Of course I googled them after our little orgy. 'They don't need this headache any more than I do.'

We'd laughed about it over hangover breakfast. How disastrous it would be if anyone found out.

Famous last words.

Charlie nods slowly, considering it. 'I agree, it seems unlikely. The hotel did a sweep. None of their staff were involved. Or at least, none of them are talking.' She lets the silence hang in the air.

The temperature nosedives, and the walls seem to close in. If it wasn't the sisters, and it wasn't the hotel... Who else was there? Who else knew? A name surfaces in my head. Kit. He'd been at the chalet with us that night, holding court in the hotel bar earlier. His face flashes through my mind – that chummy grin, the way he'd clapped me on the shoulder at the bar. *'Finn, my boy. Always the life of the party.'*

'There *was* someone else.' My voice drops. 'Kit Lascelles-Finch. He was at the hotel and the chalet that night.'

Charlie's stare slits to a knife-edge. 'The baron's son?'

'Yeah.' I drum my fingers against my thigh.

Theo's typing on her tablet. 'What's his angle, do you know?'

'Money? Boredom? The man's a human bin fire with a trust fund.' I scrub my scalp, chasing any logical thought. 'He's a party pal. And we've got history. Not all good history.'

'Define not good,' Charlie insists.

'He washed out of the academy. I didn't.' I shrug, but there's nothing casual about the tension scaling my neck. 'Plus, I might have shagged his sister at his birthday party. Two years in a row.'

Theo stops typing. 'Charming.'

'It was mutual and consensual. And ages ago.'

'So he has motive,' Charlie says. 'That's somewhere to start.'

'Aye, maybe. But I don't think he'd do it. He's a twat, but he's kind of a pal.' I glance at Theo. 'You think I'm a complete disaster, don't you?'

'No comment.'

'Okay.' Charlie coughs softly, resetting the room. 'The agenda. Theo, the Valentine's pitch?'

Theo taps her screen, her professional mask snapping back

Rucked Up Ruse

into place. 'The *Sunday Post* is interested in a "Power Couples of Scottish Sport" feature. It's a soft-focus fluff piece. Home life, shared interests, how you support each other.'

I cough out a sound that's only a half-laugh. 'Our shared interests are me being a pain in the arse and her making lists about it.'

'I can spin that,' Theo says without missing a beat. '"He's the chaos, she's the calm. A perfect balance." Readers love that dynamic.'

'Do they?' I watch the way her tongue darts out to wet her bottom lip as she concentrates on the screen.

'This isn't a joke, Finn,' Charlie says. 'The fake relationship is helping. But it's not helping enough.'

My smile falters. 'What do you mean, not enough? We held hands in public. I bought her a coffee. Smooching and all that.'

'The press is still circling,' Charlie continues. 'Leadership's spooked. The board wants reassurance. And as I mentioned, we're losing clients.' She scans from me to Theo. 'We need a bigger gesture. Something that feels undeniable.'

Theo's fingers are poised over her tablet, but she's gone still. 'What kind of gesture?'

'Okay, listen. One of the top UK lifestyle magazines wants an exclusive with the both of you,' Charlie says, dropping the words one by one. 'Feature piece. Big spread. The works.'

I feel a flicker of relief. 'Right. Great. We can do that. I'm painfully photogenic, as you've noticed.'

Charlie gives a tight smile. 'They're thrilled. But they don't just want a story. They want a *home* story.'

I take a bite of shortbread. The crumbs catch in my windpipe, and I cough – a dry, hacking sound that fills the suddenly silent office. A home story. My home is a revolving door of takeaway cartons and laundry I haven't done in weeks.

Beside me, Theo turns into a statue carved from ice.

Charlie hits the spacebar on her keyboard once, waking the screen. 'They want to see the loved-up couple in their natural habitat. The cosy nights in, the shared mugs, the whole domestic fantasy.' She lets the idea settle, a toxic cloud in the clean air. 'So. Finn, I suggest you move in with Theo. Temporarily.'

My heart thuds and breath stalls as if the floodlights have just cut out. Move in with her. With Theodora 'no comment' MacMickin. With her things. Her bed. Her wandering around in a towel.

I wonder if a man can die from a raging boner. Seems medically plausible.

'For a week or so,' Charlie adds, as if that makes it any less insane. 'Enough to stage some photos, let the press believe this is serious. Convince them you're a reformed man in a committed relationship.'

I open my mouth to say something. Anything. A joke, a protest. Even a scream. But no sound comes out. My gaze drifts to Theo. Her knuckles are white where she's clamping onto her tablet. Her perfect, serene mask has glitched, and for a second, I see the panic underneath. It's the same expression she had when I got the cut during the match.

'I'm not sure that's a good idea,' she says calmly.

'We won't do it if you're not on board. Your call.' Charlie's expression doesn't change. 'But why not?'

'I don't think we need to escalate this all the way to cohabitation.' Theo's words are clipped.

I glance at her. 'Honestly, I wouldn't let me move in with me either.'

'It's our best shot at getting the feature,' Charlie explains. 'Which is our best shot at keeping Dalcrieff off Finn's back. And that's our best shot at stopping more sponsors and clients from pulling out.'

'A week?' I ask.

'You showing up for a shoot and then disappearing the

next day, no one buys it,' Charlie says. 'But give us seven to ten days of breakfast runs, blurred selfies, you in her doorway half-dressed? That sells the redemption arc and domestication, on socials and otherwise.'

Domestication?

A thick silence descends. I hear the hum of the air conditioning, the distant city traffic. We're both trapped. The shame from before returns, hot and acidic. I don't want to invade her home. But Theo's a strategist. She's weighing the fallout and making a call, the same way she always does.

'Why can't we rent an Airbnb?' Theo asks. 'Or a fake house? We could stage it.'

'Because they want to do the shoot in two days,' Charlie replies. 'We don't have the time or resources to find a suitable location, vet it, and dress it to appear authentic. This is Edinburgh, everything is always booked way in advance. I'm not pushing it on you if you don't want to, but your flat is perfect. It's real and lived-in. It tells the story we need to sell. And we can't risk anyone finding out that we're faking it.'

My flat is also real and lived-in. Lived in by two rugby gremlins who mostly eat takeaway and Pot Noodles.

'My place is tiny,' Theo argues in a last attempt.

'It's cosy,' Charlie counters. 'The photos will look credible. But only if you're okay with it.'

Theo closes her eyes for a beat. When she opens them, she's calm and collected. A woman about to add a PR stunt to her to-do list and schedule the clean-up later.

'Okay. A week,' she says. 'My rules. And no underwear or dirty socks left on the radiators.'

The gear change nearly knocks me over. I'm so relieved I could cry. I'm so terrified I could bolt. Instead, I hear myself say, 'I promise to respect your space. But…what if the underwear is yours?'

Theo's head whips around, her eyes blazing with a fire

that's part fury, part something I can't name. But it definitely makes the air crackle.

'Jesus Christ, the two of you.' Charlie rubs her temples.

Theo isn't seeing the rugby player or the PR disaster. She's seeing the man who's about to invade her life. The chaos agent she's just agreed to let through her front door.

And her expression is unnervingly unreadable.

I hold my breath, waiting for the explosion. For Theo to retract her offer, to tell Charlie where to shove her feature piece. But she just sits there, a statue of furious composure, that impassive gaze fixed on my face. She's calculating all the ways this could go south, all the ways I could ruin her cosy life.

She's not wrong to.

My brain is a car crash of thoughts. At least seven days in her space. Her toothbrush next to mine. Her scent on the pillows. Her in a sleeping shirt with nothing underneath…

She's saving my arse. The least I can do is not be a complete walloper about it. A week – I can handle that. I can pull myself together and be a good boy. It's not that I haven't squatted before. Just nowhere with nice fluffy throw pillows.

'Right,' I say. I cough once, buying a beat. Then I try again. 'I'll be on my best behaviour. Promise. I'm an excellent house guest. You'll barely know I'm there.'

Theo makes a small, disbelieving sound.

'Okay, you'll definitely know I'm there. But in a good way. Picture a labradoodle. Enthusiastic, loyal, occasionally chews the furniture.'

Charlie pinches the bridge of her nose. 'Finn. Go home and pack a bag. Be at Theo's tonight.' She turns her gaze on Theo. 'Please send him the rules. I imagine there will be a list.'

Theo gives a stiff nod. She's staring at the glass wall, at the reflection of the three of us in this office. A ticking bomb and his two jittery bomb disposal experts.

Rucked Up Ruse

My chair screeches away as I stand. The meeting is over. The deal is done. I'm moving in with Theodora MacMickin.

Chapter 11

Theo

If cleanliness is next to godliness, my living room slash kitchen is currently a candidate for sainthood. I have scoured this flat within an inch of its life. The cushions on my mustard armchair are fluffed, the spice jars are still in alphabetical order. And since I'm giving Finn the bedroom, my electric friend, the Rabbit, has been safely relocated to the bathroom drawer.

Also, I picked out my safest jammies for later: pink flannel dotted with tiny strawberries. They scream 'wholesome' and 'do not touch'. My force field against the home invasion by Sexy MacSwagger.

It's not that I don't want him here.

It's that I want him here too much.

Even Elvis, my ginger cat, has been brushed into a state of statuesque fluffiness. He now regards me from the top of the bookshelf with a twitching tail and a mild grudge.

'Don't glower at me like that.' I wipe a non-existent smudge from the coffee table.

He yawns, revealing a pink cavern of feline judgement.

My flat is my castle. A curated space of retro prints, scented candles, and calm. It's a shoebox, but it's mine. Now,

Rucked Up Ruse

I'm about to let a human hurricane through the door. A six-foot-two Captain Chaos with pink hair and a scent that I know will cling to the upholstery and walls for days. I also know I'll have to fight the urge to press my face into his cushions and get high on it.

That's the real problem. Not the potential for mud on my rug or wet towels on the floor. It's the thought of his addictive scent embedding itself in my space and body and brain.

The suggestion of Finn moving in earlier today triggered a spike of panic that nearly took a crowbar to my composure. But I held it. I learned long ago, in a house that tiptoed around my mother's moods, that a still surface is a safe surface. My job was to be the quiet harbour. Gil reinforced the lesson. My feelings were inconvenient, my reactions 'too much'. So I locked it all behind my teeth.

Showing Charlie and Finn that the idea of him in my home made my pulse jump? Never ever.

A stack of Pot Noodles sits on the kitchen counter as an offering to the handsome God of Mayhem. I'd stared at them in Tesco for a full three minutes, feeling absurd. But it's a strategic deployment of snacks to make him feel less awkward. If that's even a thing for him. I don't know. But it is for me, so…

I check my reflection in the hallway mirror. My hair is in a neat bun, and my face is scrubbed clean. I'm wearing grey leggings and an oversized Aran jumper. Not even lipstick.

Part of me feels like a child again, making myself smaller, quieter, trying not to take up too much space in case I upset the delicate balance of the house. Now I'm wary of him taking up all the space in mine. If I'd known that this would be the cost of saving my job, I might have applied to fill shelves at Tesco.

Who am I kidding? Of course not. This job is my life.

The buzzer screeches at 6:58 pm, two minutes before the agreed time. Finn Lennox, a man whose entire brand is built on a disregard for rules and schedules, moves in two minutes early. I clock the detail. It's a deliberate act, an olive branch of sorts.

My heart trips, catches, tries again. I press a hand to my chest, commanding it to behave. It's seven days. I've survived worse. Taking a steadying breath that does absolutely nothing to steady me, I walk to the door, flick the lock, and pull it open.

And there he is.

He fills the doorframe, a riot of pink hair, dark joggies, and a plain black t-shirt that stretches across his chest. Behind him is an expensive Louis Vuitton suitcase.

But that's not the important thing.

No, the important thing is that he's holding a ludicrous armful of snacks. A multi-pack of crisps that could hide a toddler, a box of Jaffa Cakes. My gaze snags on the tub he's balancing on top of the crisps. It's a family-sized bucket of my favourite mint choc chip ice cream. The one from the Italian place down the road that costs a fortune.

I'm melting. Pun intended.

He must have asked Charlie. The thought is unnerving and thaws something that I've kept frozen for a reason.

Finn offers a hesitant, lopsided grin. The stitches in his eyebrow pull slightly. 'Snack flatmates?'

A real smile breaks through my defences. It's small, but it's there. 'Come in before you drop it all.'

I step back and he manoeuvres himself and his baggage into my hallway. The space immediately shrinks by half as he takes off his trainers. Elvis lets out a brief hiss from his perch on the bookshelf. I get it. Finn is an invasion of the senses.

'Nice place.' He scans the open-plan living room and kitchen. 'Very tidy.'

'It has to be because it's so tiny.' I close the door and the click sounds final.

'Naw. It's cosy.' Finn sets the mountain of snacks down on

my kitchen counter. 'This is the main event, I take it?' He gestures around the room.

'This is it. Living room, kitchen.' I point to the armchair and the sofa. 'You can take the bedroom,' I say, too quickly. 'My bed's bigger. Better for someone with...you know, muscles.'

'That's not happening. It's *your* bed.'

'Don't be noble. It's the only decent mattress in the flat.'

He pauses. 'Are you calling me fragile?'

'I'm calling you a professional athlete. Your spine's an asset. I'm not getting you benched because I made you sleep on a cheap coil-sprung death trap.'

He gives me a look. 'Theo. I get tackled into turf by lorry-sized mutants with no necks. I'll survive your Ikea pull-out. In fact, it's going to feel like a cloud.'

'No, it's lumpy. I sit in meetings and at my desk. Only one of us needs proper lumbar support. You're taking my bed.'

Finn saunters over to the sofa and flops down with a theatrical groan, making my meticulously plumped cushions gasp for mercy. 'This is a five-star resort. My lumbar feels fully supported. Cared for. Cherished.'

'I'm serious, Finn.'

'So am I. I've survived much worse.' He stretches his long legs out and man spreads the shit out of my tiny living room. 'See? Comfy as fuck.'

'I'm not letting you martyr yourself on my shitty couch.'

'And I'm not kicking you out of your own bed like I'm some kind of diva.'

'You *are* a diva. The biggest one I've ever met.'

'Only on Thursdays. Tonight I'm a gentleman.' He folds his hands behind his head, smug as hell. 'Look at me, being gallant.'

'No, you're being ridiculous.'

'I'm taking the sofa bed, List Girl. End of.'

'Okay, fine. Whatever.' I nod toward the closed door off

the hall. 'That's my bedroom. And that,' I jab a thumb at the other door, 'is the bathroom.'

He's watching me as if he won something. I cross my arms, refusing to let him fry my executive function any further by his mere presence in my home.

'Listen, Theo. I'm aware this is a massive pain in the arse for you. I'll try not to be a total nightmare.'

'I appreciate the effort.' Now is the time. I grab the laminated sheet from the counter. 'To that end, I've prepared some rules.'

I hand it to him and he takes it, his fingers brushing mine. A spark zings up my arm and I snatch my hand back.

He reads the title aloud. '*House Rules for Temporary Cohabitation*.' His lips twitch. 'So official. Did you use a special font?'

'Just read it, Lennox.'

'*Rule one: shoes off at the door.*' He glances at his own socked feet. 'Check. I'm already acing this. *Rule two: no houseguests.* There's zero room for any houseguests if we're both here at the same time. *Rule three: do your own laundry, we're not mixing our delicates, and I'm not your maid.*'

'Most definitely not.'

'*Rule four: always knock.*' His attention drifts to the bedroom door, then back to me. 'Goes without saying. But *Rule five: no sleeping nude* might be a problem.' A slow, wicked grin takes over his face. 'I can't be faffing about with jammies.'

'Oh, you'd better faff,' I say as firmly as I can.

'You're a tyrant, MacMickin. A cute, terrifying tyrant.'

He's trying to put me at ease. To turn my rigid list of anxieties into a joke we can share. That's his thing. And damn him, it's working. The clamp in my gut unspools a fraction.

Elvis decides he's seen enough. He leaps gracefully from the bookshelf via the chair, landing on the rug with a thud. I brace myself for the usual display of hostility. The hissing, the flattened ears, the slow, menacing tail-swish he reserves for all visitors.

But he just trots forward, tail up like an antenna.

Finn goes still, watching the cat approach. Elvis circles his legs once, and rubs his face against Finn's ankle with a startlingly loud purr.

I stare, speechless. My cat has defected.

'Well, hello there, handsome.' Finn reaches down slowly, letting Elvis sniff his knuckles before stroking him, from the top of his head to the tip of his tail.

Elvis arches his spine into the touch, his purr escalating to the volume of a small engine. He promptly flops onto his side, exposing his belly. A sacred act of trust he has never, not once, bestowed on a stranger.

I'm floored. 'Elvis doesn't do that.'

'Doesn't do what? Demand affection from devastatingly handsome men? Seems like a smart cat to me.' Finn grins and scratches Elvis right under the chin.

My cat's back leg starts to twitch in ecstasy.

'He…hates everyone,' I say, still staring. 'He actively despises other humans. I've seen him draw blood for less than risking a glance at him. Ask the plumber.'

'Maybe he knows I'm one of the good guys.' Finn's voice is soft, his attention fully on Elvis.

He's turning my cat into a wanton belly rub slut.

I watch them, this beautiful calamity of a man and my cute little demon, and something inside me melts. It's a reckless, unwelcome feeling, like the first leak in a dam. He didn't only bring the right ice cream. He tamed the beast. It's a superpower I didn't know he had, and it's ridiculously attractive.

I click my tongue, dragging my thoughts back to practicalities. 'Have you had dinner yet?'

He lifts his head but doesn't stop stroking Elvis. A brave man. 'No.'

'Okay.' I gesture to the counter. 'I bought Pot Noodles. I assumed that might be your thing.'

His eyes crinkle at the corners. 'You know me so well. Or, how about some ice cream?'

A pause hangs in the air, filled with the sound of Elvis's purring.

'How about both?' I suggest.

A wide grin splits his face. 'We're going to get on just fine, List Girl.'

And that's how I find myself sitting at my kitchenette table ten minutes later, a steaming pot of chicken-flavoured noodles in front of me, while Finlay Lennox sits opposite, happily tucking into his own. The bucket of mint choc chip sits between us, two spoons already sticking out of it. The scene is absurd. It's a photograph of a life I don't have, with a man who shouldn't be here. His knee brushes mine under the table.

He doesn't pull away.

Neither do I.

The ice cream tub is half-empty. For the last twenty minutes, we've talked about nothing. Rugby stats. My questionable taste in seventies detective shows. The structural integrity of Jaffa Cakes. It's been…easy.

Until my brain, the ever-present project manager, kicks back into gear. 'We should get some content.' I push the last spoonful of mint choc chip around the tub.

Finn has moved on to scratching Elvis's chin. 'Content?'

'A little appetiser before the main course of the magazine feature.' I stand and start clearing our mess, a sudden need for activity. 'Show, not tell, and all that.'

'You want to take a selfie together?' He sounds amused.

'I want to stage a photo that is effortlessly candid and screams "happily ever after".' I turn from the sink, and wipe my hands on a tea towel. 'It'll give the press something to chew on that isn't your arse.'

His grin is slow and appreciative. 'You're an evil genius.'

'I know.' I nod towards the sofa. 'Sit and try to appear comfortable.'

He obeys, sinking back into the cushions, and pats the space beside him. I shake my head. 'No. We need to up the stakes.'

I take a breath. This is a strategic manoeuvre. I walk over, my heart thumping a protest. I turn and lower myself onto his lap, arranging my legs so I'm sitting sideways, one thigh resting over his. The world tips sideways for a second. He is dense and muscular beneath me, radiating heat that seeps through my leggings.

His hands hover in the air for a second, uncertain. 'Where…?'

'Waist,' I instruct, my voice impressively calm. 'Gently. Like you belong there.'

My breath jams halfway at his touch, and a flaming zing barrels through my centre. He pulls me a fraction closer until my back is flush against his chest. I feel the thud of his heart against my shoulder blades.

'Okay?' His voice is a low rumble by my ear.

'Yep. Fine.'

That's a stone-cold lie. I'm the opposite of fine. I'm a system overload, every nerve ending firing at once. Underneath the sheer panic, there's heat rising up my spine. The sense of being held and protected and so, so close to…*him*.

It feels good enough to wreck my judgement.

I angle my phone to find the right frame. My hair has come loose from its bun, a few strands falling around my face. Finn seems almost possessively tender. His mouth is a breath from my neck, his gaze soft in the phone's screen.

It's a perfect lie.

'Smile like you're enjoying this,' I murmur.

'Not easy when I'm trying to keep you at a safe distance.'
'Safe from what?'
'Let's say...you've seen it in certain leaked photos.'
'Huh?' It takes a second. 'Oh.'
'Aye, oh.'

Oh god.

I'm almost sitting on his dick. I've been a few inches away from it this whole time and now I know it and he knows I know it and my brain is fried.

I stiffen. Pun *not* intended.

But why would he... I mean, I'm not his type. Even though he says he doesn't have a type, I'm definitely one hundred per cent not it.

He lets out a low breath. 'Relax, it's okay. Nothing's going to happen. It's just a reaction to how...convincing you are.'

Something about his voice makes me believe him; he sounds more amused than anything else. Finn Lennox. Rugby wild child and bad boy extraordinaire. The Dennis Rodman of Scottish rugby, so to speak. And I—

Anyway, back to business. Right the fuck now.

I snap the picture. And another. Then I scramble off his lap before my body forgets this is all performance. The air in the room is charged. I stare at the photo on my phone. It's disgustingly convincing.

'We're getting good at this.' His voice is a little rough.

'We are.' I clear my throat, eager to get back on safe and neutral territory. 'But we should probably practise a bit more. For the shoot tomorrow. We need to act natural.'

'Practise?' He raises an eyebrow, that crooked edge already curling at his mouth. 'What did you have in mind? Please say more lap-sitting.'

'Shut up. No, watching a film.' I ignore the heat that fuses my cheeks. 'On the sofa. Together. Get used to physical proximity.' I sound like a malfunctioning, overheating robot. 'As friends and colleagues, of course.'

Rucked Up Ruse

'So we're friends, now?' His grin widens. 'I'm honoured, Theo. A real promotion.'

'Don't let it go to your head, Lennox. It's a temporary post with a strict probationary period.' I scroll through the streaming services on the television. 'What do you want to watch? And if you say a rom-com, I will smother you with a cushion.'

'God, no. My heart couldn't take the schmaltz.' He thinks for a moment. 'What about *Life of Brian*?'

I stop scrolling and turn to him. Monty Python. Of course. It's absurd and brilliant. 'Always look on the bright side of life?'

'It's thematic,' he says with a shrug.

A real laugh escapes me. It's rare and wonderful. 'Fine. But I'm not singing along.'

'We'll see.'

I pull the sofa bed out to give us more room. We pile it with cushions, and I grab the woollen blanket from the back of my armchair. He sits, those strong legs making themselves at home. I hesitate, then sit beside him, leaving a careful, professional six inches between us.

He takes in the gap and smiles. 'Come here, darlin'. You said physical proximity.'

'Yeah, I remember.'

Being close to him is a bad idea, I know that. My body doesn't. It perks up like it's been waiting for this. Silly body. This isn't about wanting; it's about work. Practice.

I shuffle closer until my hip is pressed against his. He lifts his arm, and I lean into his side, resting my head on his shoulder. He drapes his arm around me, his fingers toying with the sleeve of my jumper.

It's awkward for all of ten seconds.

Then he settles, and I settle. The blanket is cosy, and the room is quiet except for the opening credits of the film. He strokes hypnotising, soothing circles on my arm with his thumb.

Elvis leaps onto the sofa, pads directly onto Finn's lap, circles twice, and collapses into a purring ball of fur. I'm flabbergasted. My traitorous cat is now seriously snuggled up with the intruder. Finn lets out a content little rumble, a low vibration that I feel through my entire body. He shifts slightly to accommodate the cat, his arm tightening around me.

'See? The whole family's here.'

My brain fumbles for a foothold, for an argument, a reason to pull away. This is not real. It's a means to an end. But my body isn't listening. My body is sinking into him, lulled by the movement of his thumb and the rhythmic purr of my cat.

Humans benefit from occasional, non-threatening touch. It's a socio-biological fact. I'm merely fulfilling an evolutionary need. It's safe, I tell myself. It's safe because it doesn't mean anything.

On the screen, a man is being hailed as the fake messiah. Here on my sofa, I'm being held by a real man who feels like salvation, and tonight, I let myself believe the lie.

The credits roll, the jaunty whistling tune that feels entirely too cheerful for the sudden silence in my living room. I am no longer just a woman watching a film; I am a woman watching a film with Finlay Lennox sprawled on her sofa bed, my cat asleep on his thighs, my hip welded to his.

I untangle myself, the loss of his warmth is immediate and unwelcome. 'Bedtime, I think.'

Finn stretches, and it makes the muscles in his arms bunch under his T-shirt. Elvis grumbles in protest.

'Aye, captain.' Finn gingerly moves the cat onto a cushion. 'Bathroom's free?'

'All yours.'

He nods, gets up, and disappears inside, closing the door

behind him. I start folding the blanket to restore order. I hear him moving around in there, the dull clack of the toilet seat, the squeak of a tap. It's all so normal. So domestic. And slightly weird.

The bathroom door opens, but I don't look up from my vigorous cushion-plumping.

'I was looking for the towels.' His voice is different. It's laced with a specific kind of amusement.

I turn slowly.

He's leaning against the doorframe, holding my Rabbit as if it's a priceless archaeological find. It's bright purple, unmistakable, and currently the sole cause of my impending death by spontaneous human combustion.

My brain ceases all function. My mouth opens, but only a small, strangled squeak comes out.

'Found this little fella in the drawer under the sink,' he continues with that smug, shit-stirring sparkle in his eyes. 'Seems friendly.'

'Give. Me. That.' The words are a low, furious hiss. And the heat on my face could power the whole grid.

He doesn't move, just inspects it with a connoisseur's eye. 'It's a classic. Good choice. Reliable motor, I've heard.' He throws me a gaze with an infuriating glint that means he's having the time of his life. 'Self-care is important, Theo. Good for you.'

He says it with such breezy sincerity that I'm momentarily disarmed. There is no judgement in his tone, only cheeky approval. Gil would've recoiled, wounded pride and quiet disappointment. He'd have said something like, *'I didn't realise you needed that sort of thing.'* Followed by sighs and a silence that said I'd let him down. It would've become another thing I kept hidden.

God, I'm so glad we never lived together.

But Finn's acceptance invites closeness I am not prepared for.

'It's for…muscle tension,' I ramble.

'Aye, I bet it is. The best kind of muscle tension.' He strolls forward and places it gently on the small coffee table, as if it's a perfectly normal appliance. 'Night, little guy.'

My composure has been reduced to rubble. I march into my bedroom, shutting the door. When I emerge a few minutes later in my clean and wholesome strawberry-print jammies, he's in the bathroom, shirtless, brushing his teeth. The air carries the scent of mint and him. He's already made the space his. I grab my own toothbrush, determined to reclaim my territory. We stand side-by-side in all our domestic glory. I spit into the sink, the sound loud in the small room. I risk another glance at him in the mirror. My brain supplies a vivid, unwelcome fantasy. It's a detailed, high-definition daydream of his mouth replacing my vibrator.

The thought hijacks my brain and makes my knees weak.

I need to get a grip. This is the man whose dick was a national news item and who's now sleeping on my sofa bed as a PR stunt. The probability of my fantasy coming true is lower than the chance of the real messiah descending upon humankind.

Finn rinses and spits, catching my eye in the mirror. He's not smiling. He saw something on my face, the flicker of the daydream.

Then he leans closer, his voice a low murmur. 'For future reference: I've got a lot more settings than him – and much better angles.'

Chapter 12

Finn

I wake throbbing with it. The dream still clings to me. Theo's lips, bare of their usual red. She'd opened for me, blue eyes locked on mine as I pushed against the plush resistance until she took all of me. The memory makes my cock twitch against the thin cotton of my boxers.

Jesus fuck.

The flat is a furnace, Theo must run her heating at tropical levels. I kicked the covers down sometime in the night, leaving me sprawled across her sofa bed in nothing but black boxers that are doing a piss-poor job of concealing my current situation.

I don't even *have* jammies. But at least I'm not naked.

Elvis is curled by my feet.

I hear a soft gasp. It's not the cat.

I open another eye, squinting against the morning light flooding through the curtains. Theo stands stock-still in the doorway between the hall and the living room, dark hair loose around her shoulders. Her gaze is riveted to my boxers, lips parted in surprise. Her pupils flare.

She likes what she sees.

The thought sends a fresh pulse of heat straight to my

groin. I reposition slightly, not hiding my reaction but not flaunting it either. It's enough to let her know I'm aware of her presence. Nothing to be ashamed of.

'Mornin',' I rasp.

She startles as if I've fired a gun. 'I was—' She tips her chin toward the kitchenette. 'Matcha…erm…or coffee?'

'Caffeine in any form sounds brilliant.' I stretch, arms above my head, and notice how her eyes follow the flex of muscle.

'One sex…erm, sec. Oh god.' Even her ears flame. She puts space between us fast and ducks behind the counter.

I grin at the ceiling. The woman who plays pool like a pro and handed me a laminated list of rules, is undone by my morning glory. It's hilarious, fucking sweet, and deeply, viscerally satisfying.

She's banging around in the kitchen area, clattering with mugs and spoons. Aye, she's flustered. Theo MacMickin, professional problem-solver, is rattled by my cock – which, to be fair, is standing prouder for her than a piper on parade.

Perhaps I should feel bad. I don't.

Perhaps I should get up, throw on a shirt, play the gentleman. I don't do that either.

Instead, I lie here, listening to her moving around, imagining her hands shaking slightly as she measures coffee. Imagining those same hands on my skin. Between us. On me. The dream wasn't enough. The sleep-mussed reality of her makes the throb so brutal that it might split me in two.

Elvis yawns, stretches, and pads over, head-butting my chin with a loud purr. The kettle clicks off. She's still loitering by the sink. I have exactly two options: get up now and risk derailing her further, or stay put and torment us both.

I'm a rugby player. Careful, sensible choices? Not our thing.

. . .

Rucked Up Ruse

Shortly before the interview, I'm in the exact same spot again. This time, fully dressed and no longer showing off a tent. Miracles happen. But my chest's gone tight again. My mind's revving like we're in a final scrum. Ten minutes until the magazine crew arrives. Ten minutes to go from 'has been escorted out of three nightclubs' to 'devoted domestic boyfriend with media training'.

I need to splash water in my face. I need to...

The bathroom door is ajar. She must've forgotten I was here. Or maybe she never bothers fully closing the door, habit of living alone. Did she mean to leave it open...?

I drift forward before I think better of it, pulled by heat and awe and the ghost of her shampoo.

Theo stands with her back to me, wearing nothing but a black lace bra and a matching scrap of fabric that clings to the curve of her magnificent arse. It's round, high, and soft in a way that blows every thought clean out my skull. My hands itch with the urge to grab. I want to kneel, to press my mouth there, and earn the right to stay. I don't know how I'm supposed to move, speak, exist, with that view in front of me. It takes everything I have to wrench my eyes up and will my dick down. I only succeed with number one.

Goddammit. I should back out and apologise. I should do anything except stand here, staring at her like I've been booted out of heaven and someone left the door cracked open to tempt me back in.

She catches my reflection in the mirror. 'Fuck, Finn! I told you to bloody knock.' Her voice is edged with embarrassment, but it falters at the end. Too breathy to pass for anger.

'Sorry.' The word comes out rough. I take a step back, finally, guilt chasing down my spine.

She bites her bottom lip and presses her thighs together, just slightly, as if she's trying to shut the moment down from the inside out. Her cheeks reach a new level of beetroot, but it's her eyes that catch me. Dark, deep, and wide. She's breathing harder now, nipples tight against the lace. There's no hiding it. It's *need*. And now she doesn't have time to conceal it.

'Get out,' she says, but there's no force behind it.

'Say it like you mean it, and I will.'

'Finn, I…'

'Do you want me to leave?' I make a step forward.

'N-no.'

We're close enough now that I see the pulse fluttering in her throat.

'The dress.' She nods to a navy blue hanger on the back of the door. 'I need help to get dressed.'

I reach for it, the fabric is smooth under my fingers. Hips, curves, everything about her is screaming for me. How she moves, how her body begs to be touched, and I'm fucking dying to. She steps into the dress, her back still to me. I hold it open, and my fingers brush against the skin of her waist as she slides her arms through.

'Zip up, please,' she whispers.

I gather her hair and place it over one shoulder. The nape of her neck is exposed, goosebumps rising on her skin. My fingers find the small metal tab at the base of her spine. I draw it upward, watching the dress close over her back, inch by inch. Her inhale stalls the second my knuckles graze her spine. I take my time. The zip stops just below her shoulder blades. I let my hand linger there, feeling the heat of her skin, the raised hair.

I lean forward until my mouth is next to her ear. 'There.'

Her shivers ripple under my palm. It's making me lose my mind.

'Thank you,' she says softly, but she doesn't move away.

Neither do I. We stand suspended in this moment, my fingertips coasting across the bare stretch of her upper back. I could turn her around, kiss her, pin her against the sink, and hike that dress up her thighs…

Rucked Up Ruse

The buzzer shatters the silence.

She jumps as if electrocuted, and steps away from me. 'They're early.'

'They're bastards,' I correct, my throat tight around it.

Theo smooths her hands down the front of her dress, a gesture of composure-gathering, straightens her shoulders, and lifts her chin. I watch her transformation with awe and frustration as professional Theodora slots back into place.

'Ready?' she asks.

No. I'm not fucking ready. I'm the furthest thing from ready. I'm hard and aching and desperate to peel that dress right back off her soft, inviting, stunning body. To bury myself in her.

But I make myself nod. 'Let's give them a show.'

She steps past me. 'That's what we're good at, isn't it?'

The question hangs in the air, loaded with more meaning than either of us is ready to unpack.

The doorbell rings again, more insistent this time.

I follow her out of the bathroom, watching the sway of her hips in that navy dress. No, we didn't cross the line yet. But we sure as hell blurred the shit out of it.

While the journalist scribbles her notes, I turn to Theo, who's perched on the arm of her mustard chair. Her hair's up in the usual high ponytail, all shine and swing. Hard not to think about pulling it backwards, while I…

It's going smoothly. Theo's been a revelation. Sweet, thoughtful, the perfect girlfriend. A performance so convincing it's making me question my sanity.

'That's it,' the photographer coos. 'Now Theo, lean in a bit. Like you're about to tell him a secret.'

Theo moves closer and her knee brushes mine. The contact lights me up from the inside, hunger licking through my system – that low, dirty pull I've been trying not to feed. Her eyes meet mine, and my chest goes tight in that way it does around her. As if she's reaching into something I didn't give her permission to touch but let her anyway. I've never felt something even remotely like it. And fuck me, for half a second I want to kiss her and stake my claim right there in front of the whole damn crew.

'Perfect!' The camera clicks rapidly, and the photographer seems happy.

'Now Finn,' the journalist asks, 'tell me again what drew you to Theo initially?'

I've answered this question three different ways already. Each time, I've dug deeper, said more than I meant to. Some form of truth is seeping out between rehearsed lines.

'Other than she's the prettiest girl in Scotland? Her competence.' I don't break eye contact with Theo. 'She walks into a room and everyone knows she's got it handled. And she doesn't take any of my shite.' I pause, watching her pupils dilate slightly. 'I love how she sees through the rugby rebel act.'

'Mmm, that's sweet.' The journalist keeps writing in her old school notebook, phone recording on the table beside it. 'And Theo, explain again what made you forgive Finn after the scandal?'

Theo's smile softens. She finds my fingers and holds my hand. 'He's so much more than his persona or his mistakes,' she says. 'He owns them, he's trying. That's rare in a man.'

My chest locks up. She's so bloody good at this. I almost believe she means it.

'One last shot,' the photographer announces for the third time. 'I want you both on the sofa. Finn, sit normally. Theo, could you sit on his lap? I want you to look at him as though he's the only man in the world.'

We rearrange ourselves. Theo settles on my thighs, angling her body towards mine. Her hand rests on my chest, right over my thundering heart. She must feel it, the way it's trying to break through like it's charging a try line.

'Now look at each other,' the photographer instructs. 'I want to see the connection. The intimacy.'

Theo's already watching me, blue eyes wide and unguarded. For nearly two hours, I've been telling strangers how much I adore this woman. How she grounds me and makes me want to be better. How there's no one whose opinion matters more to me, no one I want to make laugh more than her.

And as I stare into her eyes, the words echo back with weight I didn't expect. The truth burrows under my skin. I wasn't faking a single syllable.

'Super!' The camera clicks again. 'The chemistry between you two is electric.'

I disagree. It's not electric. It's a fucking power grid meltdown.

Theo's gaze drops to my mouth for a fraction of a second. Her lips part slightly. The hand on my chest curls, fingers bunching my shirt. A tiny, involuntary movement.

Real. That was real.

Unless it wasn't. Unless she's just *that* good.

Too good for me in a million ways.

'I think we've got it,' the journalist announces, and closes her notebook with a satisfied snap. 'You two are absolute gold. The redemption angle, the forgiveness, the moving in together – it's a perfect escapism story for our readers.'

Narrative. Story. Fiction.

Theo's hand falls away from my chest. The loss is physical, cold rushing in the second she lets go. If I didn't know any better, I'd say my body's still reaching for her.

'Thanks for being so generous with your time,' the journalist adds. 'The feature will run next week. We'll send copies, of course.'

Theo stands, smoothly transitioning into hostess mode. 'Can I offer you both another coffee before you go?'

'No, we should get back to the office,' the journalist says, and gathers her things. 'But thank you for welcoming us into your home. It's been lovely.'

Lovely. What an inadequate word for the riot that's been raging inside me all morning.

The two women leave in a flurry of thank-yous and polished smiles. The door closes. A hush drops, thick and suffocating.

Theo leans against the wall. 'That went well.'

'Aye.' My voice sounds strange to my own ears.

She pushes off, and brushes past me to start tidying the living room. 'They seemed to buy it.'

'They weren't the only ones.'

She pauses, a cushion in her hands. 'What?'

I scrub a hand over my face. 'Nothing. Just knackered. Have to go to training.'

She sizes me up for a moment. There's a wariness in her eyes, a careful distance that wasn't there during the interview. The performance is over, the curtain has fallen.

'You were good,' she says finally. 'Very convincing.'

'So were you. Oscar-worthy, in fact.'

She smiles, all surface. 'That's the job, isn't it? Making people believe.'

A job. Right. That's all this will ever be. What a wee shame.

Sure, I told myself I wouldn't drag her into my mess. But I'd be lying if I said part of me didn't want to throw every rule out the window, pull her in, and see what fucking happens.

Chapter 13

Theo

The time is 3:33 am, and everything feels wrong. The sudden, absolute silence of the flat is what woke me. No hum from the fridge, no electronic glow from the router.

Brilliant. Another power cut.

It's freezing. A deep, penetrating cold has settled into my bones and makes my teeth ache. And I'm a human icicle because my good winter duvet is currently cocooning the flanker on my pull-out sofa.

For four days after the interview, it's worked. We've existed in the same flat on different schedules. I wake to the lingering scent of his shower gel; he gets home from late training to a note about the recycling.

His days revolve around rugby. Early mornings spent at the gym, followed by perfecting drills, running through contact scenarios on the pitch. If it's a hard week, he's at the physio, getting his muscles loosened or dealing with niggling injuries. I, on the other hand, work late into the evenings, dealing with deadlines, clients, and schedules. It's an unspoken avoidance strategy. A necessary retreat after the photoshoot.

The things he said during that interview replay in my

head. *'How she sees through the act.'* He'd looked right at me, his gaze stripping away the polished layers of the girlfriend persona, straight to the woman underneath who was panicking. A perfectly executed lie that rang uncomfortably true.

I have a serious Finn-shaped problem. A problem that has moved from my sofa into the part of my brain that's supposed to handle logistics and long-term planning.

I'm just gonna admit it.

I like him.

It's an inconvenient, unprofessional, and frankly foolish development. But there's nothing I can do about it.

I really, really like him.

A soft thud from the living room, followed by a half-screamed, fractured groan.

Every muscle tenses, ready for... I don't know what. I lever myself out of bed until my bare feet hit the floorboards. Then I stand and inch forward, my hand flat against the wall for guidance in the dark.

The living room is bathed in the faint glow of a full moon that has found a gap in the clouds. It's enough to see Finn. He's tangled in my duvet on the pull-out, half-sitting. The unicorn sleep mask has slipped up from his eyes to his forehead. His breathing is an erratic rhythm that cuts through the silence. His eyes are wide, staring at a spot beyond me.

He's drowning or something. In the middle of my living room, he's drowning.

My heart pounds so hard it bruises my ribs, and my brain flashes through a list of anxieties.

This is too much. This is how you get burned. This is...

But my feet are already moving. My instinct to fix is a force of nature. This old reflex is stronger than my fear.

And this is not anyone. It's Finn.

I don't make a sound until I'm right beside the sofa. 'Shhh...Finn.'

His head snaps towards me, but his eyes don't focus.

Rucked Up Ruse

They're glassy with terror. He's not here. He's in another world, somewhere awful.

'Hey...' I keep my tone gentle and even, a human stabiliser. 'Hey, it's me. Theo.'

I don't ask what's wrong. I don't ask if he's okay. He is clearly *not* okay, and the question is useless. Instead, I pull back a corner of the duvet. I budge in beside him, my strawberry-print jammies the wrong uniform for this kind of rescue mission.

No idea if this is one of those 'do not wake up' or 'wake up immediately'-nightmare scenarios. So I'm going with my instincts. They're all I got. I roll onto my side to face him and carefully pull him towards me. The space is so tight that our knees are bumping. I lift my hands to his face. His skin is clammy.

'You're here with me.' My voice is a quiet line in the dark. I turn his face towards mine, forcing him to see me, to latch onto something real. 'The power's out, that's all. But you're safe. You're here.'

His pupils are vast, black holes swallowing the moonlight. He's looking through me. A shudder racks his body.

'Hey. Hey, look at me.' I stroke his cheek lightly. 'I've got you. I'm here.'

I place my palm flat against his sternum. His heart is a wild beast trapped behind his breastbone.

'Feel that? That's my hand. You're safe. It's okay.'

He gasps, a ragged sound, and his own hands fly up, tangling in my hair. It's not rough or harsh, more a clutch. A drowning man grabbing a rope. His fingertips press against my scalp, rooting himself in the reality of me. Of us.

'Breathe with me, Finn.' I take an exaggerated breath in, hold it, and release it slowly. 'Come on. In...and out.'

His gaze flickers, a tiny spark of awareness.

'Again,' I command softly. 'With me. In...' I watch his chest rise in a stuttering, shallow movement. 'And out.'

He lets it go in a rush.

'Good. That's so good.' I start a rhythm. 'I'm right here. You're not alone. It's okay. It's okay, love. I'm here.'

His breathing starts to slow, to match my own. The wildness in his eyes begins to recede, and his focus sharpens until he's not looking through me anymore. He's looking *at* me. Seeing me.

The woman in the silly jammies who crawled right into his nightmare.

The erratic pounding of his heart beneath my palm eases and settles into a heavy, resonant thud. We're inhaling the same cold air, exhaling the same small cloud of steam. We're breathing each other.

'Sorry.' He sounds sandpaper-rough. 'Bad dream.'

'Yeah, I figured as much.'

He traces the shell of my ear with his thumb, so featherlight it tickles. 'You shouldn't have to deal with this. You need sleep.'

'Neither should you. Yet here we are.' I don't move away. The pull between us has its own gravity, so elemental that it makes physics irrelevant. 'Wanna talk about it?'

He swallows, the sound audible in our cocoon, and lets the silence settle. I think he's weighing whether unloading all of it is worth it or not.

'My... My da died over Christmas, a day after my birthday. Overdose. In The Big Hoose – Barlinnie. Didn't even hear until days after, when I got a birthday call from my oldest sister.'

I blink. 'Shit. Finn. I'm so sorry.'

He shrugs as though it's nothing, but tension rolls off him. His chest is tight again. Not panic this time. Shame, I guess.

'I didn't go to his funeral because I didn't truly know him. Hadn't talked to him since I was eleven. He left when I was wee and got done for dealing and other stuff a few years later. Wasn't exactly a loss, but... Still fucks you up and makes you wonder what part of you wasn't worth sticking around for.'

I don't speak. Just let him keep going, because he needs to.

'My mum didn't want a boy. Not one like me anyway. She had two daughters already, from another father. The better one, I guess. I was the accident. Loud and hyper. Got into fights and broke stuff. She used to say I came out wrong. That I gave her headaches. That I looked like him.'

A muscle under my heart pulls taut. He says it as though he's reading a weather report.

'She'd slap me when I got mouthy, ignore me when I got quiet. I learned early on that if I wasn't making her laugh, I was making her mad. So I got good at the first thing.'

'Christ,' I breathe.

'She kicked me out when I was sixteen. Caught me nicking a perfume from Boots because we had no money. I was gonna give it to her for Christmas.' His voice doesn't break – it buckles, as if each word hits a bruise on the way out. 'She lost it. Called me a thief and a liar. Said I'd end up like my da.'

I bite the inside of my cheek. He's not crying, but I might be. 'You stole her a present, and she threw you out?'

'Aye. Didn't speak to her after that. Crashed at a mate's for a while. Slept in a youth hostel a couple nights. On floors. Sometimes outside. Didn't tell anybody. School was fucked, but rugby…'

I stay still and move my fingers over his chest, drawing quiet outlines only he can feel.

'Rugby was the only thing I didn't mess up.'

'Tell me about it.' I think the pitch is where he feels safe, so I take him there. 'How did it start?'

'I've been playing since I was nine. I didn't know the rules, didn't care. But I liked smashing into things and being told I was good at something for once. After Active Schools came a club, then trials, camps. Academy. I didn't have the grades or the gear or the parents with cars, but I kept showing up, and I kept winning them matches. That's the main reason they didn't toss me out. When shit hit the fan, they eventually gave me kit and food and a bed in a host family's house in Edinburgh.'

My chest knots around the ache to make it better. I want to kiss every awful memory out of his skin. But I can't, so I run my hand down his chest.

'You want to know the worst part? I kept hoping she'd change her mind. That one day, she'd let me come home.' His voice holds, but only just. Every word is flattened into armour, every pause is a seam that wants to split. 'I was sixteen, Theo. Sixteen and standing in the cold thinking if I made it big enough, she'd want me back.'

His inhale shudders. Not a sob, but it rips through me anyway. I've never heard him speak without that protective layer of charm and bravado. This is Finn stripped bare, and it's more intimate than if he'd shed every stitch of clothing. The power cut has plunged us into near darkness, but I see him perfectly. I reach for his face. My fingers graze the curve of his jaw, then settle over his cheek. Steady, so he knows I'm not pulling away. He turns into my touch.

'I'm so, so sorry Finn. She didn't deserve you then. And she definitely doesn't now.'

The faint moonlight catches his eyes, turning them silver-rimmed. I can count his eyelashes, see the scar above his eyebrow that the stitches will leave behind.

We're nose to nose, and I feel the moment his focus shifts to my mouth. Every unspoken word, every near-miss, every fake touch that wasn't fake at all… It all crowds into the small space between us.

'Theo.'

He stays perfectly still, letting me lead, letting me decide.

This is no surrender. It's a choice made in the frozen, moonlit quiet of my flat to lean into the one thing that is warm and real.

Rucked Up Ruse

He traces a line from my temple to my cheek. The pad is rough, and it drags heat across my skin like flint catching spark. My body leans into the touch before I can stop it. My breath slows and stops altogether.

We're about to kiss.

Oh, yes. Yes!

His lips graze mine, soft and devastatingly gentle. Not at all what I expected from the man who never shuts up. There's reverence in it. My lips barely touch his. Finn exhales a shaky breath through his nose. He hadn't expected this either.

I kiss him back, because there's no oxygen otherwise.

His mouth is warm against the chill, slightly chapped, tasting of toothpaste. I flatten my hand on his chest, and our hearts are beating with each other. One pulse, one need. A single, breathing entity, hiding from the ghosts in the dark.

He finds the back of my neck with one hand, and settles the other down to the small of my back, pulling me closer until there's no space, no question, no way out. His stubble scrapes against my jaw, and static sparks under my skin. His hand tightens slightly at the base of my skull, as if he's afraid I'll disappear. I hold on to his shoulders. He's the only stable thing in a world that's going sideways.

God, yes.

His mouth catches mine, tongue teasing at the seam as if he's asking. I part for him, and the kiss breaks open – electric, all-consuming, blisteringly intense. His lips soften, coaxing mine wider until his tongue meets mine in a stroke that I feel in my toes.

No, in my fucking *soul*.

He tilts his head to find that perfect angle. A slow sweep, tasting every part of me he's allowed. His hands stay where they are, but his delicious thighs tense against mine. His whole body has gone still. He's holding himself in place, refusing to chase more than I give him.

He learns the shape of me, I learn the depth of him. And I want it. The real him.

He licks into my mouth with purpose now, deeper, pulling me with him. My tongue meets his in a slow drag, and it's sweet and overwhelming and everything. We don't battle, we *fuse*.

He makes a hoarse sound, and the pressure of his body against mine surges – more urgent now, as if he's losing the fight to stay gentle. I bury my fingers in his hair to bring him closer, closer, closer and he groans. So low and guttural that it hits me right in the chest and sinks lower. Lower and deeper and—

We break apart just enough to breathe. Our foreheads touch. I don't open my eyes. I can't. His exhale is hot and trembling against my chin.

Another kiss. Then two more. There's no start or end now. Only this moment and this impossible, beautiful truth of us being safe together in the dark. He slides his tongue in as deep as I let him and it's still not enough.

His breath melts into mine when he draws back far enough to look at me. There's a blaze in his eyes, but there's something else, too.

'I'm not done kissing you,' he says. 'That was the first. The first of many.'

A beat drops hard beneath my breastbone. There's a pulse between my legs that won't stop, and the damp lace clinging to me is a quiet confession my mouth hasn't made yet. But it's his promise that unravels me.

This was always going to happen, and I'm only catching up.

He leans in again, lips ghosting over my jaw, my cheek, the corner of my mouth. Each contact is a slow drag of possession.

'I need you to understand something, Theo. If you're not ready to end up on my cock tonight – tomorrow, whenever –

then you need to leave now. Because I am *this* close to snapping. And if I fuck you, it's not going to be once. You won't walk straight. You won't think straight. And I won't be sorry.'

A moan catches at the back of my throat.

His gaze dips between us, and his mouth curves. 'Your nipples,' he trails his fingers down the outside of my arm, 'are clearly on board. Fully invested. You? Not so sure. I want you to be ready, Theo. Make a pro and con list if you have to and let me know. Cause I'm game.'

I should say something. Anything. But I'm too far gone. There's a hot, slick ache at the centre of me that throbs in time with his words, and I want to climb him. I want to argue, I want to laugh. But mostly, I want to feel him inside me.

He presses a kiss to my temple. Tender and at odds with everything else.

'Thank you for being here tonight,' he says. 'You didn't have to be. But you are. I'm not going to forget it.'

That alone undoes me more than anything else. This is the blood-red danger zone, and I'm in the centre of it.

What am I doing?

'Okay, yeah. No problem. Night then.' I wriggle out from under the duvet, fleeing the crime scene.

Every inch of me is lit and fevered, bursting with unsaid yesses. The hallway spins. Or maybe that's just me, walking on legs made of custard. I stagger to the bedroom, shove the door shut behind me, and press my back to it like I'm barricading something in. Or out. Who knows.

I'm soaked – not cute-wet, disgracefully-wet – and aching in places I can't soothe.

I fling myself into bed and yank the duvet up to my chin, trying to remember how to breathe like someone who hasn't just been kissed half mad and is about to combust from unsolicited, inappropriate horniness. My mouth's still wet from his, my chin is sore. Every part of me feels too full and nowhere near satisfied.

A few minutes with my trusted Rabbit, and I'll sleep like a baby.

I reach for the drawer and pause.

Oh no.

Oh no no no no. It's still on the coffee table in the living room. Next to the remote. I shove my face in a pillow and quietly scream into it in frustration. Then I flip onto my back and stare at the ceiling like it holds the answers.

'Make a pro and con list if you have to and let me know.'

I don't need a list or bullet points. I know what I want. But I don't know what wanting him means or what it'll cost me. If I say yes to this, it's not a shag or an itch. It's opening a door I've kept bolted for ages and letting someone like Finn step through.

I bunch the duvet in my hand.

'I'm game.'

Jesus, Mary, and Joseph – I think I am, too.

Chapter 14

Finn

I've stopped fighting the hard-on. That's life now, sharing space, leftover pizza, and daily life with Theodora MacMickin.

Have I fantasised about her lips like a teenage boy with broadband for the first time?

Aye.

Did I think kissing her would rewire my entire nervous system?

Fuck no.

But it did.

Four days after that night and she's barely acknowledged me since, as if she's afraid I'll read her mind. Or worse, she'll read mine.

I'm a desperate man. But at least I think I'm not alone in that. She's taken the Rabbit back to the bedroom.

Christ, I'm fucking aching when I think about her hips grinding up, thighs braced wide, the Rabbit pinned between them. Head tipped back, lips trembling, coming hard with my name stuck halfway to a moan.

I've got a bowtie slowly strangling the last of my common sense, and still, all I can think about is her coming. What the hell is this with us? There's only one thing I know for certain: it's not fake anymore. If it ever was.

I'm sitting on the edge of her sofa in a rented tux, sweating through the shirt and praying she doesn't walk out in something that'll finish me off.

I'd fuck her through the wall if she'd let me. Hard and fast or slow and deep, over and over. But I also want her curled up against me after. My nose in her hair. Her breath on my neck. I want to spoon-feed her ice cream and lick it off her tits. I love how she takes a beamer each time she realises that I saw her hard nipples through the cotton of her sleeping shirt. Jesus, I want to spend the rest of my life on this sofa bed with her and Elvis and die a happy man.

It's like my heart is having a boner. And that's new.

It's also stupid. Far out of my comfort zone – and way out of my league.

Theo's the sort of woman who owns nice mugs and pays a mortgage. She's got a brain as sharp as a scalpel and eyes that could slice through steel. She gets things. Not only facts, but people. She watches me as if she's working out the angles and sees the cracks I've spent years trying to plaster over.

And I keep forgetting to be scared of all of that.

Because when she kissed me back, she didn't hesitate.

I've never been kissed like that. Her lips… Lush and swollen. The first contact was all heat, a soft, slick drag that caught on the seam of my mouth. Her breath hitting the back of my throat just before her tongue flicked out. One slow glide, barely inside, to taste me and make me chase her for more. Her lip caught between my teeth. I didn't bite, didn't dare, but I thought about it. Thought about what she'd do if I did. My cock throbbed in time with the pull of her mouth, and I swear I forgot where we were. All I knew is that I was safe and powerful, full and hungry at the same time.

She made me feel this way.

Rucked Up Ruse

I know, it's all happening fast. But at the same time it feels as if it has already happened, has always been this way.

Now I'm supposed to get through an entire black-tie gala without thinking about that mouth. That kiss. That noise she made when she opened for me. Christ. That night... She listened. Didn't jump or run. Just held me. For the first time in – I don't even know – I didn't feel like a fuck-up or a disappointment or a half-moulded version of a man. I felt wanted.

But that feeling? It's a slippery bastard. And it's been four days. She hasn't brought it up. Maybe she's changed her mind and regrets it. Or she kissed me like that because she was sorry for me.

Naw.

Except...maybe.

I keep telling myself it's nothing and I'm reading too much into it. But my brain's got a sick sense of humour and a long memory. And this woman – this perfect, sharp-edged, soft-curved miracle – she could break me with one look if she wanted to.

So I'm playing it cool. Sitting here in this monkey suit, fiddling with my cufflink like I'm not seconds from losing my grip.

Then I hear the soft pat of her bare feet on the floor. My head snaps up.

It's not a dress. It's a fucking trap.

Pale green, almost silver in the light, the silk flows over her like it's got somewhere to be. Every inch clings. Hips, waist, tits... There's nothing hidden and nothing asking for permission. It doesn't hug her curves, it celebrates them. One side of her dark hair is clipped back with an antique silver hair comb, showing the line of her neck. The rest spills over her shoulder in shiny dark waves. When she turns, the silk pulls across her arse like it's holding on for dear life. Every step sends it stroking her thighs, smooth as poured cream, tempting as fuck.

Holy hell.

I think my heart just came in my shirt.

I blink, trying to focus on anything but her dress, her.

As if.

She fumbles with her earring. 'You clean up nicely. Very Bond.' Her voice wavers on the last syllable.

Christ, she's nervous – and it floors me like a tackle I didn't see coming.

I get up, the tux suddenly feeling too tight, too formal. 'Wow. You are...' I trail off, shaking my head. My vocabulary shrinks to caveman grunts when faced with her looking like that. 'That dress should be illegal.'

I follow her into the hallway.

'I'm gonna say only one thing, Theo.' I let my breath skate over her ear as I help her into her coat. 'I'll have to fake fuck all tonight.'

Stirling castle is a fairy tale come to life. Purple and gold lights on the stone walls and timber beams of the Great Hall. The SRU's Burns Night Fundraiser is apparently a full medieval fever dream, hosted by some bigwig from the Scottish Rugby Union I've already forgotten the name of. Judging by the line-up of sponsors, donors, and the number of kilts paired with Rolexes, this isn't exactly your local pub ceilidh.

Long banquet tables stretch down the middle of the hall, all deep green fabric, silver cutlery polished enough to check your teeth in, and flower arrangements bigger than grown men's torsos. Pink roses, purple thistles, dark green ferns.

The whole thing kicked off earlier with a piper and the *Selkirk Grace*, followed by the *Address to a Haggis* delivered by a bloke who went full theatrics with the knife. He practically stabbed the poor thing into submission.

Now we're between courses and halfway through the

speeches. Someone just quoted *A Man's a Man for A' That* with full chest.

Charlie and Brodie are across the way, eyes following everything with a hint of wariness. Can't fault them for it. Her dickhead of an ex-fiancé is here, beaming with his shiny new wife-to-be. A TV presenter or something. Brodie's always a bit murdery in a crowd, but tonight he's dialled to Maximum Menace. Charlie matches him glare for glare in a red velvet number that could start fights on its own. They look ready to sack a city.

Scottie hasn't said a word. Just looms, brooding into his whisky like the glass insulted his maw. That's atypical. He probably misses living with me. James keeps twitching his phone on and off, barely glancing up. If he gets one more text, I might hurl it into the Forth myself.

And then there's Theo, sitting next to me, close enough to smell her perfume. She hasn't said much since we arrived, but I can sense her. Every breath. Every time her fingers tense against her napkin. Back straight, shoulders tight, eyes scanning the room.

So I lean in, enough for our shoulders to brush. 'Relax, List Girl. The worst is almost over.'

I rest my hand on the top rail of her chair as if I've done it a hundred times. No one's watching us right now, but it doesn't matter. I do it anyway, in case they are. Or in case she needs it.

Her hand loosens in her lap. 'I swear, one more speech and I'll stab the cake fork into my ear.'

I laugh. And because I'm a wee rascal, I also kiss her temple.

'Finn!'

'All for the show, darlin'.'

A new suit takes the podium at the top of the hall. He's grey at the temples, with the kind of sombre face that tells you the fun part of the evening is over. If there ever was such a thing.

'Tonight isn't only about celebrating Robert Burns or our sport,' he begins, his voice echoing in the hall. 'It's about remembering why we're here. What we're donating to. This year, we lost a bright talent. A young man who fought battles far from the pitch.'

The air in the room changes. The cheerful clatter of forks and glasses goes quiet.

'Liam Kennedy was a warrior for his club. But he struggled in silence.'

The name hangs there. I remember him, a winger from Glasgow. Fast as lightning. Died last spring, far too early.

'We're here to raise awareness for mental illness among brilliant athletes. Depression kills.'

Next to me, Theo goes rigid.

And it's not a subtle change. It's a total system shutdown. One second she's a breathing woman in a dress that could make a monk break his vows; the next she's a marble statue. Her hand, resting on the table, curls into a fist so tight her knuckles are white peaks. She's stopped breathing, I'm sure of it.

My own chest constricts. Fuck, I know that expression. The one where you leave your body so you don't have to feel what's happening inside it.

My hand finds her thigh. Not for the crowd. For her. I hope it's an anchor. I squeeze gently, a silent question. She doesn't flinch, doesn't even seem to notice. Her violet eyes are pinned on the speaker, but they're blank and vacant.

'We're here to ensure no one else feels they have to face that darkness alone,' the man continues. I should remember his name, but I can't. Middle-aged white dudes all look the same to me.

I catch a strand of her hair between my fingers, twirling it

Rucked Up Ruse

once. 'You with me, MacMickin?' I keep my voice a low rumble.

Nothing. She's a million miles away.

The speech ends with a call for donations and a moment of respectful silence that feels anything but silent. It's full of shuffling feet and awkward coughs. Full of ghosts.

My hand is still on her leg. She's still not here.

'Theo.' I say her name again, firmer this time. I give her thigh another squeeze. 'Breathe, baby.'

She finally gasps, a sharp, quiet intake of air, as if she's just broken the surface of water. Her gaze snaps to mine, wide and panicked. There's a universe of fear and pain in them. A raw terror that has no place at a black-tie dinner.

The clinking resumes as the crowd returns to eating, but the mood has curdled. A stocky man in his late sixties with a face carved from granite and opinions sits three seats over, whisky glass in hand. That one, I recognise instantly. Coach MacGill, the dinosaur who ran drills at my first academy camp.

He gestures broadly. 'Everyone's bloody depressed these days, aren't they? Got a ragged cuticle? Depression. Girlfriend dumps you? Depression. In my day we didn't have the luxury to stay in bed all day and cry about it. We sucked it up and got on with the job.'

Two men next to him burst out in a half-suppressed laugh. Next to me, Theo's breathing accelerates to shallow pants. Her pupils dilate until the blue is nearly gone.

'I need air,' she gasps, pushing back from the table so abruptly her chair scrapes across stone. 'Sorry. I need—'

She's gone before I can stand, weaving between tables toward the door.

I'm on my feet, but MacGill's voice halts me. 'See what I mean? The kids can't handle a bit of truth these days.'

White-hot rage floods me. I plant my palms on the damask. 'That's what killed Liam Kennedy.' My voice drops to a growl. 'Your generation's "suck it up" and "boys don't cry" bullshit is why that lad's in a coffin and not on the pitch.'

His face flushes purple. 'Now listen here—'

'Respectfully, sir, go fuck yourself with that attitude.'

I leave him spluttering and follow Theo's path. The corridors of Stirling Castle are a maze, but I catch a flash of silk disappearing through a doorway to an outside terrace.

Eventually, I find her leaning against the stone balustrade above Queen Anne Garden, arms wrapped around herself, shivering in the January cold.

'Theo?' I approach her slowly. 'Mind if I join you?'

A small shrug. She's shivering. I take my jacket off and drape it around her shoulders. 'Wanna talk about it?'

She stares out at the towering, ornate silhouette of the Wallace Monument. My jacket swallows her. Can't believe how small and raw she seems now. Her arms are wrapped tight around her waist. I lean against the cold stone next to her, giving her space and don't push. The muffled sound of laughter drifts from the hall.

I'm about to say something daft, but her voice cuts through the quiet. 'When I was thirteen, my mum stopped getting out of bed.' Her tone is flat and even. 'She's okay now, but for years the situation was tough for all of us. Volatile.'

I stay silent. My job right now is to shut the fuck up and listen.

'She wasn't sad or anything,' Theo continues with her gaze fixed on the dark horizon. 'Not in the way people think. She's a sculptor and used to say she could see the outline of things inside the stone. And one day, she couldn't anymore. It was just stone. Her inner light went out.'

I press my hand flat to the balustrade.

'My dad's job was charting the seabed for the Royal Navy. He was away more than he was home. I told him something was wrong. That Mum wasn't eating, that she only stared at the wall.' She takes a shaky breath. 'He got angry. Really angry with me. Told me I was being dramatic, that I was imagining things. That I was never, ever to mention it to anyone outside the house. After that, he left for a survey that took six weeks.'

The rage that was simmering for MacGill finds a new, hotter target. Her father. 'So you were alone with her?'

'I was scared she was going to...die. And that it would be my fault for not fixing it. My grandparents had passed. I had no one. No one checked in or even noticed.'

Jesus Christ. She was a kid, holding a collapsing world together with her bare hands while the man who was supposed to help her told her she was crazy. My own teenage years feel like a holiday compared to that. Well, almost.

'I started cooking. Paying the bills online from his account. I found where she hid the gin. The box cutter from her studio. I hid all the knives.' She finally turns to me, and her eyes are two bottomless pools of old pain. 'I became a good fixer.'

I see it then, all of it, and everything clicks into place. The lists, the way she handles chaos without breaking a sweat. It's not a personality trait. It's chain mail, forged in a quiet house by a thirteen-year-old girl who learned that if she wasn't in control, her entire world would shatter. Her mum could die. And she'd be the one left to clean up the pieces.

Good god. The word 'fixer' is too bland for what she's describing. It's like calling a bomb disposal expert a handyman. All this time I've seen the polish, the precision, the laminated lists, and thought it was simply who she was. An organised, slightly bossy, brilliant woman.

I was wrong. It's the shell she crafted around herself as a girl. Built in silence, under pressure. And fuck, it held.

'Theo.' My voice is scraped raw by everything she said.

Her eyes are swimming with tears that she's fighting to hold back. She's still trying to contain the damage.

'That's not being a fixer,' I say. 'That's being a soldier.' I take a step, closing the space between us until my shoes are touching the hem of her gown. 'He was wrong. Your da. He was so fucking wrong.' I reach up, my thumb brushing away the track of her tears. 'You weren't being dramatic. You were being abandoned, and you learned how to survive.'

Her breath catches on a sob she refuses to release. Her whole body trembles inside my jacket. I can't bear it. I can't bear seeing her like this, so broken and so strong all at once. I gather her into my arms and pull her against my chest. She resists for a second, then she folds into me, and I forget how to breathe. Her body against mine, all the fight gone out of her. She presses her face into my pecs, hands clutching the lapels of my jacket. A silent, gut-wrenching series of shudders that rack her frame. A grief so deep it has no sound.

I lock my arms around her, rest my chin on the top of her head, and breathe in the scent of her hair.

I'm holding thirteen years of fear in my arms.

The rage I felt before was a spark. This is a fucking inferno. I want to burn the whole world down for her.

Her sob finally breaks, a raw sound muffled by my shirt. The dampness spreads against my skin.

Good. Let it all out, baby.

'I've got you,' I whisper into her hair, the words feeling small and useless against the scale of her pain. 'I'm here, my darlin'. Just breathe.'

I hold her, my fingers sinking into the soft waves of her hair, protecting her from a world that's done its worst. We stand there on that cold stone terrace, a two-person island in a sea of bullshit and kilts.

The polished, perfect Theodora MacMickin is gone. In her place is this trembling, heartbroken girl who's more real and more beautiful than anyone I've ever known. And I'm the one she fell apart with. The thought is both scary and humbling.

She pulls back to look up at me. Her face is a mess. Mascara smudged beneath her eyes, cheeks tear-stained, lips puffy. She's never been more heart-stoppingly beautiful.

Rucked Up Ruse

'Sorry.' She tries to wipe her eyes with the back of her hand, a gesture of someone trying to pull the armour back on.

'Don't you dare apologise.' I catch her hand and stop her. 'Don't you ever fucking apologise to me for your feelings.' I use my thumbs to gently wipe away the black smudges from under her eyes. 'We're leaving,' I state. It's not a question.

'Finn, we can't. The charity. Charlie…'

'Fuck the charity. And fuck this whole goddamn castle.' I keep my hands on her face, forcing her to meet my gaze. 'I'm taking you home, baby.'

For a moment, she looks like she might argue. I see the fixer trying to reassert control, to do the sensible thing.

Then, a small, exhausted dip of her chin. 'Okay.'

The relief that washes through me is so intense it almost knocks me off my feet. I keep one arm on her waist as we walk back inside, a line of defence. We rush through the crowd, my hand a firm pressure on her lower back, guiding her in the direction of the exit.

Charlie's gaze finds us across the room and her smile dies. One glance at Theo's face and she's halfway out of her seat. I shake my head. *Not now.* Brodie registers it too, his gaze narrowing on Theo's face before flicking to mine. He gives me a short nod. *Go.*

We don't stop for coats. We don't say goodbye.

My girl needs out. So I'm taking her home.

Chapter 15

Theo

There's a man in my kitchen wearing a tux who's arranging biscuits into a castle.

This is not a metaphor.

The same man who drove me home from Stirling Castle. The same man who stripped off my heels, unzipped my dress, and helped me into my oversized hoodie without his hands straying once.

I'm watching Leith's streetlights flicker through the bay window, swaddled in the chunky knit blanket Gran made me when I was a girl, shortly before she passed away. My face is tight from dried tears, but the panic has receded, leaving behind only exhaustion and a hum of comfort in my chest.

Finn just witnessed me detonate. A full, snot-and-tears implosion. And he didn't back away, didn't call me dramatic, or try to patch me up with empty phrases. He listened, got me the hell home, and put the damn kettle on.

He moves around my tiny kitchen space with efficiency. His bow tie hangs loose around his neck, shirt sleeves rolled to his elbows. The tux trousers hug his thighs as he stretches to reach the biscuit tin I keep on the top shelf. Thighs built for scrums and sin.

Rucked Up Ruse

'Want shortbread with your chocolate digestives?' he asks without turning.

'Of course.' My voice wavers a bit. 'I'm emotionally compromised, so calories don't count.'

The soft sound of his low laugh fills the quiet flat. Elvis weaves between his ankles, purring like a motorboat.

Wee weirdo.

We didn't speak on the way back. I stared out the window while Finn drove, his hand occasionally squeezing mine at red lights. No questions or platitudes. Just his presence.

He brings over a mug of hot chocolate topped with mini marshmallows and a plate stacked with biscuits.

'There. Dig in.' He plants the plate on the coffee table. 'Biscuits are a key part of any post-meltdown debrief.'

The care in this simple act cuts right through my defences. He puts it in front of me like it's no big deal. But it hits somewhere deep, where no one ever bothered to look.

'Thank you. For getting me home.'

His little finger grazes mine as he passes me my favourite glittery mug. The contact sets off a chain reaction. Something sparks under my skin, like someone lit a match inside my bloodstream.

He sits down beside me. 'I'd have carried you out over my shoulder if needed.'

'That would've been a dramatic exit.'

'Aye.' He dunks a shortbread finger into his hot chocolate. 'MacGill can rot in hell, by the way.'

I take a sip. 'You didn't have to defend me.'

'More defending basic human decency.' He scratches the back of his neck.

I've forgotten what it feels like to let another person take some of the weight. I'm not even sure I've ever known this feeling until this very minute.

'You know what's mad?' I watch the marshmallows melt.

'I've never told anyone that story before. Not any of my friends, not Charlie, nobody.'

'Why me, then?'

This matters. Why him? Why the rugby player who drives me mental and makes me laugh and kisses me like the world's ending and he wants to take me with him?

'You showed me yours first,' I say simply. 'Your scars. That night with the power cut.'

He nods and reaches for my hand, strong fingers lacing through mine on instinct. 'We're quite the pair, aren't we?'

'Disaster recognises disaster, Lennox.'

'Speak for yourself, MacMickin. I'm a goddamn delight.'

I laugh, and his eyes crinkle at the corners, pleased with himself for teasing it out of me. I watch him with a sideways glance. Pink hair growing out at the roots, the newest scar is still red across his brow, stubble darkening his jaw. He's undeniably hot. But he's a lot more than that.

Finn didn't run when I unravelled. He saw the ugliest, messiest version of me and his first instinct was to make sure I was safe. And my brain, the overthinking, list-making, control-freak part of me, goes completely still. A thought lands with the clarity of a church bell on a Sunday morning.

Finn is lovely.

In fact, he might be the loveliest man I've ever met.

I've been keeping him at arm's length because vulnerability has always been linked with pain. But with him, it isn't.

He reaches across me for another biscuit. His skin smells of the cherry soap I keep by the sink and something muskier. Heat hits the backs of my knees and climbs fast.

Control has been my currency since I was thirteen. I've been holding back out of habit, out of fear, out of a fierce need to stay upright in a world that keeps shaking under my feet without warning. But this man walks straight through every firewall I've ever built. And I don't know if that scares the shit out of me or sets me free.

Maybe control isn't what I need right now.

Maybe it's Finn.

Yeah, it's definitely Finn.

I set down my mug and bring our intertwined hands to my mouth, pressing my lips against his knuckles.

'Thank you,' I say, barely louder than the soft whir of the fridge.

His eyes darken as I kiss his hand again. Slowly, I drag the tip of my tongue across the galloping pulse in his wrist.

'Fuck's sake, Theo…'

His eyes flare as I let go of his hand to peel myself from the blanket. His gaze sweeps over me, taking in my hoodie and bare thighs. I see the battle in his eyes, the war between desire and restraint.

'Theo, you've had a hell of a night. I'm not going to take advantage of your vulnerable state by—'

I cut him off with a smile, and lean in until our noses almost touch. 'Stop being so noble, Lennox. If anyone is taking advantage of my vulnerable state right now, it's me.'

His brows shoot up, surprise and fire in his expression. 'So I take it there were more pros than cons on your list?'

'Oh, I didn't even make one.'

This is revolutionary. I've made lists for everything from which university to attend to what brand of toilet paper to buy. But not for this. Not for him.

I place my hands on his shoulders, and his muscles are tense beneath my palms.

'Last warning.' His hands hover at my hips. 'When we're doing this, we're fucking doing this. And not just once.'

I move, swinging one leg over his thighs, then the other, until I'm straddling him. 'I sure hope so.'

'Fuck.' The word drops between us. 'Are you *really* sure?'

I kiss the place where his collarbone meets his neck. 'I don't do uncertainty, Finn. You know that.' The hard heat of him sears through the thin, damp lace between my thighs. I yank his bowtie away and nip his jaw. 'You still game?'

His pupils swallow the last slivers of blue. 'For you? Hell yeah.'

Chapter 16

Finn

Theo's fingers are on my buttons, and I think I've stopped breathing.

One.

Two.

Three.

Each one pushes more oxygen out of my lungs. She's straddling me as if she's claiming what's hers and done waiting for permission. Hoodie riding up her hips, bare skin pressed to my tux trousers, working a grind of heat across my lap that fucking wrecks me.

All I see is her mouth. All I want is more of it. That lush, clever mouth. The same mouth that just kissed my hand like it was sacred.

She dips her chin and peers up through her lashes. There's this tiny lick of her tongue against the corner of her lip, and I nearly lose it. It's not even a kiss, and I'm spiralling.

She leans in slow… Her mouth finds mine, and I'm gone.

Her kiss doesn't ask. It *claims*.

Top lip slick with heat. Her breath tastes like chocolate and marshmallows. I want to breathe her in, swallow her whole, and never let her out.

Theo sinks her fingers into my hair, and I groan as her mouth opens for me. I take her face in both hands to kiss her deeper, give her my tongue hard and fast. She kisses me back like she's starving, and I'm so in – wet, hot, all in.

I should pace myself.

But then she moves her hips against me and…no chance.

She rocks again, and it lands right where I need it. Slow drag over the part of me that's been begging for her. She sighs against my chin and it rips straight down my spine.

'Goddammit, Theo—'

She shushes me with another kiss.

I push my hand under her hoodie. No bra. She's soft and full in my hands, heavy enough to make me swear. I sweep my thumbs over her nipples, and she pushes into my touch as if I'd flipped a switch.

'I've thought about this.' I run my open mouth along the line of her neck. 'So many times. But it's not even close to how good you feel.'

I take that damn hoodie off her. 'I've fantasised about this a hundred times, Theo…'

'And what…did you do in those fantasies?' Her breath leaves her in a rush, and she holds the back of my neck to pull me closer.

'Tugged my cock slow thinking about how your tits would bounce if you rode me.' I give them a slow squeeze. 'And every time I came, it wasn't enough. Because I couldn't fucking touch you.'

'Then stop talking and put your mouth on me.'

My laugh breaks on a groan as she pushes against me. 'Bossy.'

'Only when I need to be.'

'Oh, I'll show you what you need.' I lean in and take one tight peak into my mouth, sucking until she lets out another shattered moan.

Every rock of her hips sends a new ripple through me. My

Rucked Up Ruse

cock is straining so hard it hurts. Her skin is silk and heat and the closest thing to heaven I've ever touched. I want everything. Every fucking heartbeat. And she's right here, letting me touch her like this. Not pretending it's anything less than raw need.

Real. This is as real as it gets.

She rolls her hips down, and the sofa's springs dig into my back like teeth. I don't give a damn. Her head falls to my shoulder, and she lets out a sweet little series of pants I'll never recover from.

'Shit, Theo... You've got no idea what that does to me.'

She gasps again when I rock up, letting her feel every ridge of pressure, every bit of friction.

'That's it, baby. Now open my trousers.'

Her eyes shoot to mine, wide and dark. 'I—'

'You heard me.' I cup her neck with my hand. 'You're soaked and I'm dying. Get my fucking cock out, Theo.'

She swallows, and I feel it with my whole body.

Her hands drop to my waist, fingers trembling. She fumbles the button. I don't help her, I watch – her concentration, how her teeth sink into her bottom lip...

She takes her sweet time with the zip, her knuckles grazing lower. The second she dips her fingers under my waistband, I swear to Christ my ribs tear open. My hips jerk up – fuck patience – and I shove everything down in one ruthless motion: trousers, briefs. My cock's free, thick and hard.

She stares and her gaze goes *hungry*. 'I knew it. Of course you're gorgeous there, too.'

The fuck's she doing making me feel shy about it? It shouldn't work on me. That shouldn't—

She closes her fingers around the base, so tentative it makes my head spin.

'I was right,' she says. 'You don't need small hands to make it look bigger.'

And just like that, I laugh – with a painful hard-on. God, this woman.

She drags her thumb over the head, catching the slick there.

'You're gonna kill me, Theo.'

She sinks forward against me again. Her hot centre glides over me, lace barely a barrier.

I let out a low, fucked noise. 'Careful or I'll come like a teenager.'

'Don't you dare.'

'Then *don't* move like that.'

But she does. Slow rolls that drive the head of me against her clit through that thin strip.

'You hear that?' I ask.

The wet sound of her arousal dragging over me. Oh, she hears it. Her whole face burns. Blushing Theo is always stunning. But blushing Theo with bare tits rubbing herself up and down my cock? That's a fucking work of art.

And Jesus Christ, I want to fuck that pink deeper.

'Don't get shy now.' I kiss along her collarbone. 'You're aroused. That's fucking sexy.'

She rubs over my entire length again, dragging fire behind it. I reach between us, nudge the lace aside, and tease my fingers through her folds, slick and hot.

'Fuck. I could slide right in, Theo.'

She gasps out a bitten-off curse, and it shoots through my bones like lightning.

'Theo, baby... You're making noises I'll be replaying in my head till I'm ninety.'

'I think—'

'Don't think. Just *feel* me.'

She bites her lip and moves. Slow, slow, slow. Up and down now.

'*There*. That. Do that again.'

She rocks her hips in a tighter circle. I drop my hands to

her arse and I yank her down, hooking my thumbs under the lace. 'You want to take these off?'

She nods again, pupils blown. 'I need you. You,' she breathes. 'Finn. Please. Now. I need—'

'Let's see.'

Her hips buck when I work my hand between us. I trawl two fingers through her hot, swollen flesh, just enough pressure to part her. She's…so soft. Smooth, and so fucking wet that the seam of her clings like a kiss. Not just slick, thick with it. My middle finger catches on her entrance, and that first scant millimetre? A molten, fluttering grip. She's alive under my hand.

I curl, find the spot, and her entire body quivers. 'Mhm… There, baby?'

A rasp breaks out of her, halfway between surrender and disbelief. I suck one nipple into my mouth. She hisses through her teeth as I strip my fingers from her and paint her lips with them.

'Open.'

Her tongue darts out, and she tastes herself, eyes blazing into mine.

'Tell me, baby – you need more of my fingers,' I cup her jaw with one hand, 'or are you ready to be fucked? Your choice.'

'I-I want…' She's hiccupping. 'God, I want everything. But I don't know how to—'

'Stand up, my darlin'.'

Eyes glaze-fix on mine. Slowly, she rises from my lap.

'Now take them off for me, nice and slow.'

She hooks her thumbs into the waistband of her panties and peels them down. They catch slightly on one thigh, then fall at her feet. She steps out of them. Soft curls, dark and natural, glossy where she's wet for me. Fucking glorious. My cock kicks at the sight.

I reach down, snatch my wallet from the trousers on the

floor, and fish out a condom. I tear the foil and roll it on with shaky hands. Her eyes track my fingers like she's memorising how wrecked she's got me.

Yeah, look close, baby. That's how fucked up I am for you.

Because this thing between us? It's not heat. It's white phosphorus behind my sternum. The high of realising she's letting me in. She's giving me the parts that never make it out of the armour. That's the real addiction – trusting me. And she's doing it with her eyes wide open. As though I'm not a problem, but the thing she wants.

Not tolerated or endured. *Wanted.*

And when I sit back, it's with wonder and gratitude and greed for more.

'You don't have to say anything right now.' Her voice goes threadbare. 'Just…please don't stop looking at me like that.'

'Not as long as I have eyes.'

'I don't know how to do this without pretending I'm not scared. But I don't want to stop.'

'Come here.'

She climbs onto the sofa, knees on either side of my thighs again.

'You don't have to pretend anything.' I grip her hips and guide her in close. 'You just have to let yourself be mine.'

And I mean it. I want the broken part, the fear and fury and softness underneath. I want all of it to be mine.

She reaches between us, and for a second, her hand hovers as if she's not sure if she's allowed.

'Aye, take it, baby. All yours.'

A ragged exhale. 'You're so…hard and…' Her teeth dig into her bottom lip.

I feel her guide me, my tip teasing her entrance, hotter and softer than anything I've ever felt in my life. She inches forward.

'Go slow, baby. You're so tight, you'll need a moment.'

She nods, fiercely focussed. But her voice is almost fragile.

'I'm trying. But I want to…feel everything. I need you so much.'

Her thighs flex and she sinks down a bit. A groan rips from my chest as if it's been buried there for years. She stretches around me with tight, gripping heat. She's letting me in – really in – and my body's fighting to hold back when all I want is to disappear inside her.

'God. Oh my god. I feel you, Finn. I…'

I haul her closer, one hand splayed up the dip of her spine, the other locked on her hip. Another slow descent and I nearly black out. The pressure steals my breath. Jesus fuck, she feels like home. Her chest brushes mine, nipples dragging over my shirt where it's still half-buttoned. She exhales against my jaw. And then she takes me all the way.

Fuck, fuck, fuck.

Her pussy is clenching so damn hard I feel her heartbeat around my cock.

She puts her hands on my chest, like she needs to hold on to something. 'Please, Finn… Don't move. Just…stay.'

I feel her everywhere, even in my fucking veins. We breathe together. Her lips part like she might speak, but doesn't. Maybe because words would cheapen it.

I stay buried and let her adjust. Let her settle.

'I need you to feel…how much I want you…' Her words break, catching halfway.

She lifts her hips and I slide out an inch, feeling the velvet drag of her heat. Then she sinks back down with a sound that knocks the breath out of me. A gasp turned moan turned fuck-I'm-dying-with-bliss.

A groan claws up my throat. She moves again, faster now. Friction and urgency and the reckless pull of being so far gone.

'Ah, Finn… Oh yes…'

She rides me like she's furious at herself for wanting this

so badly. At how it's not just sex. And yet she's moving harder, chasing it.

'It's not enough…' She sinks her teeth into my neck to muffle a frustrated whine. 'I can't… God, I need—'

'Tell me.' I swipe her hair back and catch her breath with my mouth, kissing her so deep her hips writhe.

'F-fuck me.' She digs her nails into my shoulders. 'So I feel it tomorrow. So I know this is real.'

That wrecks something in me and breaks it wide open. 'It is, baby. Never doubt that again.'

I sit up, wrap one arm around her back, the other holding her neck, and flip us in one hard motion. 'You need to be cared for. Fucked right. So let me.'

Theo nods, hands scrambling on my waist to pull me in. I lift her leg higher and drive in deep. Her mouth drops open on a strangled inhale.

'There she is, taking it all. That's my girl.'

She tries to speak but her words melt into a sob when I rock into her, slow and gentle. Her hands clutch at my shoulders.

'Still want more?' I press my forehead to hers. 'Want me to own that pussy?'

She nods, wide-eyed and wrecked. 'Yes. Yes!'

I thrust into her slow. Then hard. Her nails bite into my back when I go deep, but it's not pain she's giving me. It's proof that she wants it. And fuck me – that needy whimper when I push in again. That right there could stop my heart. And I could go on forever.

'Finn… You feel so good…'

Shit. I'm losing it. I can't fucking think. It's all wet heat and greedy muscle, dragging me in deeper with these slow, torturous pulses that have my balls drawing up tight.

'Christ. CHRIST… Listen to it. That fucking sound when I sink into you. Goddamn, baby!'

That's the thing – that's the fucking thing – this clench, like she's trying to keep me buried there forever. It's not just tight, it's *mine*. Her body pulls me deeper, taking me to the hilt like she's hell-bent to brand herself on me.

Her body *knows* mine.

She hauls me deeper with her thighs around my hips and punches out a little cry every time I bottom out.

'You... fuck... you take me so perfectly...' I'm babbling, my words slurring into growls, my brain short-circuiting because... because—

Because nothing has ever felt like this.

Not the way she moans when I graze that spot inside her that makes her toes curl. Not the way her legs lock around me like she'll die without me inside her.

Her back arches and her mouth drops open. 'Ah! Yes! Finn... Ohhh!'

I keep pounding into her snug channel, keep my rhythm, make it good for her. 'I never fucked anyone the way I'm fucking you, Theo. Baby...'

'Yes! Yes! I'm already... It's... I'm coming! Don't stop...'

'Look at me.' My voice is cracked open, like the rest of me.

Her eyes flick up. Wide, dazed. 'I...oh god, I...'

Her mouth falls open, trembling lips forming a silent o. The flush starts at her chest, climbing across her cheeks. Sweat pearls at her temple. She's glowing – *glowing* – as if I've lit her from the inside.

'Yes! N-now! Ohhh... OH!'

And she breaks.

It rips through her. Her thighs quiver around my hips, her back bows, and she clenches so tight I can't breathe. She's shaking, one hand clawing for my neck, the other still pressed to my chest like she's binding herself to my heartbeat.

Her eyes roll back to pure white. 'Finn! Finn...'

And I've never seen anything like Theo exploding around

me. I watch her fall apart. Her head tips back, the column of her throat exposed, her skin pink and shimmering.

Beautiful.

It's that fierce, rising heat flooding her that undoes me. Proof that it's real, that I did this to her, that she's not hiding from me. Not faking anything. I want to press my mouth to every inch of it.

'Can I go harder?'

'Yes, yes!'

And I do. I fuck her from her orgasm right into mine. The pressure's unbearable now, white-hot and right there. My balls cinch up.

'Theo! Fuck! Baby, I...'

She grabs my face. Eyes still glassy, lips swollen, voice broken. 'I'm here. Don't stop. Please don't stop.'

My vision whites out.

I thrust once, deep and urgent, her body's still pulsing around me. My forehead drops to hers. I need her breath in my mouth, her heartbeat against my skin.

Whatever leaves my chest isn't human. It's hoarse and helpless and full of her name. 'Theo! Ah! Theo—'

My release tears out of me with her name in my mouth and her cunt still gripping like she'll never let me go. Her name is the only thing I remember how to say, and I say it over and over as I come so hard I forget who I was before her. I groan into her skin, into her hair, into the space between us that doesn't exist anymore. My body goes weightless and heavy all at once.

Theo's still holding me, watching me as if I'm not broken or too much. As if I've always been hers. She giggles against my temple, and her fingers stroke my neck, while I'm trying to return to Planet Earth.

'What's so funny, woman?' I ask between breaths, grinning so wide my face hurts.

Rucked Up Ruse

'Nothing. It's just...' She nuzzles into my neck, voice drowsy with satisfaction. 'You said you had more settings than my Rabbit. And if this was number one, I can't wait for the other nine.'

Chapter 17

Theo

A purr loud enough to register on the Richter scale wakes me. For a dizzying second, I think it's me.

Then I open my eyes.

There's a rugby player's arm pinning me to my sofa bed, and he has my cat's arse in his face.

The grey Edinburgh morning filters through my curtains, highlighting the chaos we've made. Duvet, blankets, and sheets twisted around our legs. My hoodie crumpled on the floor beside his shirt, trousers, and bow tie.

Finn smells of my cherry soap, his own skin, and the musky scent of sleep after sex. Elvis is loafing on his chest like Finn's a brand-new, premium-grade human mattress.

My body is a roadmap of last night. A dull, delicious ache is settled deep in my bones. I still feel his mouth on my nipples, the pressure of his hips, the scrape of his stubble against my neck. I'm warm from the inside out and sore in places that haven't been sore in ages. And never like that.

I seriously fucked Finn Lennox.

This wasn't supposed to happen. It wasn't supposed to get anywhere near this real and physical and emotional.

My brain, a command centre of schedules and contingency

plans, feels like it's been put through a spin cycle. This whole arrangement was for headlines. For damage control. It was *not* for mind-melting orgasms and whispered confessions in the dark. Not for…whatever the hell this is.

A quiet, curious ache builds inside me. Last night wasn't just sex. One thousand per cent not. But what else? And what now?

I need to get up. I need a bit of distance to clear my head.

With surgical level care, I try to ease myself from his embrace, lifting his massive arm by degrees. The movement is glacial. I'm afraid to wake him up before I've had the chance to collect myself.

Elvis slits open a single green eye, glares at me for disturbing his new favourite sleeping spot, and resumes his motorboat purr.

The wee turncoat.

Finn stirs and pulls me tighter against him. I go still, trapped in the circle of his arm. His chin tucks into the space above my head. The panic rabbiting through my chest softens. My cat, who hisses at the postie, jumps any boiler man, and bit Gil's ankle twice, is using Finn Lennox as a heated luxury cat bed. And I…don't hate it. Actually, I might be melting internally –into soup with heart-shaped noodles.

Wow, MacMickin. How the mighty have fallen.

Sure, I'm still afraid. But there's something deeper under it now. A glow that spreads through me like butter on hot toast.

The Stirling Rebels' wild child flanker made me hot chocolate last night. With marshmallows. After watching me snot-sob and crumble into a million pieces. He took care of me like no one ever has, and the least I can do is return the favour.

Second attempt at sneaking out from under this arm and I'm prying myself free with the stealth of a thief disarming a security system. One leg, then the other. His arm flops onto the empty space I've vacated, and he mumbles something before burying his face in my pillow.

He's cute. I can't believe that I think he's cute. But he is.

I sit up in slow-motion, and grab my hoodie from the floor, where we dropped it last night. The memory sends a shiver across my skin that has nothing to do with the morning chill. I pull it over my head and let the cotton fleece fall to mid-thigh, enough coverage to preserve a last shred of dignity.

What dignity? The one you gave up on your back last night when you begged to be impaled by his huge rod?

The wooden floorboards creak beneath my bare feet. I wince, pausing mid-step like a cartoon burglar, but Finn doesn't stir again. His hair is flattened on one side, stubble darkening his jaw, one tattooed arm flung across his eyes. He doesn't even wear his sleeping mask. The sheet barely covers his hip, revealing the sharp cut of muscle.

I tear my focus off him to literally anything else. If I keep obsessively staring at him, I won't get anything done ever again.

I tiptoe to the kitchen area, wincing as I open the cupboard door with its tell-tale squeak. My matcha tin sits on the second shelf, nestled between the Earl Grey and the chamomile. I pull it down. Two scoops of bright green powder into the bowl. A splash of cold water. I whisk in tight W motions until the paste is smooth. It's an absurd amount of effort for a drink, I know, but the ritual calms me.

I heat the oat milk in a small saucepan, careful not to let it boil. Patience is key. Too hot and it scorches, too cool and the matcha won't bloom properly. I've perfected this over hundreds of mornings, calibrated to my exact preferences.

But will he like it?

The thought catches me off guard, this sudden concern for someone else's taste buds.

'Is that a potion to turn me into a frog?' His sleepy voice is a low gravelly rumble from the sofa bed.

I startle, nearly sloshing the matcha over the rim of the

mug. Finn is propped up on one elbow, sheet pooled around his waist, hair sticking up. Elvis has migrated to his side.

'Frog, prince... Tomato, potato.' I pour hot oat milk into the mug, and the green liquid swirls into a pale jade.

'That's not how the saying goes.' He scrubs a hand across his jaw, his gaze honing in with amusement. 'Are you hiding behind that counter again, MacMickin?'

'What?' I let out a short laugh. 'No? I'm making a beverage. It's what people do in kitchens. Matcha. It's green tea. Healthy. Lots of antioxidants.'

'Mhm.' He stretches with a yawn and the sheet sinks lower, clinging to the sharp V of his hips.

My eyes drift to the intricate ink swirling over his body, the chaotic tapestry of his life story written on his skin. Another tattoo I hadn't noticed peeks out along his hip bone.

Shit. He's so hot, it's literally unfair. What am I meant to do with all that...man in my bed?

Well... You could... Stop it!

He sits and swings his legs off the sofa. 'So, about last night...'

'Good point. We should probably talk about it.' I force my gaze back to my matcha.

'I'd say so, aye.'

I refuse to glance his way, but I hear his smirk.

'It was...erm...exceptionally good sex.' I take a gulp of matcha. 'We're unusually compatible in that area.'

'Agreed.' He saunters towards the counter, utterly unselfconscious about his state of undress.

He's very, very naked and impressive even now. I know his other state, and I'm still sore from it.

'You're blushing, Theo. Any indecent thoughts you'd like to share?' He leans against the counter next to me. Naked, mind you.

'No. Why? No.' I hand him the mug.

'Cheers.' He takes a cautious sip. 'This is actually nice.'

'So was last night… It was really fabulous sex.'

'It was really fabulous *everything*,' he corrects, voice dropping an octave.

The quiet certainty catches on something deep inside me.

'I know.' The words come out sharper than intended, so I soften my voice. 'But this is still a temporary, mutually beneficial arrangement to save both our arses. We aren't *together*-together, are we?'

'The papers think we are boyfriend and girlfriend.' He stretches again, a long, languid movement that shows off every sharp line of his torso. 'So does my team.'

I'm actively drooling over the man who is systematically dismantling my life's operating system. This is fine. Totally fine.

'And what do *you* think?' I hate that I ask.

'Last night wasn't for the headlines and neither is this morning.' He sets his mug down and comes closer. His eyes are impossibly blue in the pale morning light. 'What I think is that we are whatever we *want* to be.'

'I'm not sure I'm ready for a full-on relationship, Finn. I'm not in the right place, mentally.'

'I get it. But in another way, you *are* in the right place. You're here with me.' He steps behind me and digs his fingers into my hair, finding the worn-out scrunchie. He tugs it out and my mane tumbles over my shoulders. 'Better.'

'I have to admit, I *do* enjoy spending time with you.' The words tumble out before I can analyse them to death.

'Same.' His breath tickles my ear.

'So what the hell does that make us?' I lean back against his chest.

His lips map the sensitive spot where my neck meets my shoulder, sending currents skittering all over. 'It means we'll keep doing what we're doing, follow the plan until the last game of the season and see where we stand.'

Rucked Up Ruse

I reach back, finding the nape of his neck, and let my fingers play with the soft hair there. 'A situationship?'

He trails his hand beneath my hoodie and up, cupping my breast with his callused palm. I'm dripping and pulsing, and he's hardly even touched me. This has never happened before.

'Naw, this feels better. More exclusive.' One pinch, just shy of pain, and my nipple beads hard against his fingers. 'More like a Theofinnship.'

'That's not a real word.' I have to keep myself from panting.

'It is now.' He grazes my earlobe with his lips. 'I just invented it.'

I rock back and feel him, hard and impatient.

'Tell me...' He kisses the pulse point below my ear. 'Does that sound good, List Girl? Or do you need a full risk assessment before we proceed?'

Slowly, he runs his other palm up my thigh. The heat of it sinks into my skin. He's still behind me, hips aligned to mine.

'Okay, no. I'm good. This is good. So good.' The words rush out too fast and too honest.

I feel his smile as his touch climbs, stealing every thought except *yes, there, more.* When his hand presses on my mound, it's more than skin on skin. It's him saying, *'Feel that? That's where you're mine.'* And god, I do. Every heartbeat throbs against his hand, begging.

'Sore?' The first pass of his fingers is gentle. 'Tell me if it's too much. But don't lie. I'll know.'

I suck in a breath, eyes snapping shut.

'Knew you'd do that, close your eyes like it'll hide how much you like my hands on you. Too bad I felt you lift into my touch.'

He presses a single finger to my clit and spins the lightest circle.

My knees almost give. 'Oh...'

'Mm.' He hums like he's pleased. 'Nice?'

'V-very.'

His thumb finds a slow rhythm right on the spot that's been aching since he first kissed me good morning with nothing but his eyes.

'More?'

My hips surge forward, control be damned, chasing whatever he's about to give me.

'I'll take that as a yes.'

'Yes…'

I shouldn't want this so much. He's too good at this.

He runs his finger through my soaked centre before shoving it in. And all my thoughts scatter like dropped marbles. He moves like he has nowhere else to be, like my body's the only place for him. And I roll into his touch with shameless need.

'Already this wet for me? You're going to be the reason I skip breakfast every day.'

I spread my legs wider to give him better access, and he plunges a second finger in. A sound escapes me that I will deny under oath. My spine bows, and I grip the counter. Finn keeps playing me with his fingers. Heat races up my spine, and I'm seconds from combusting when he stills his hand.

'Hey,' I protest between breaths. 'Not…fair.'

'Since when do I play fair?' He withdraws his fingers and I gasp from the loss. 'I want my mouth on you, Theo. I want to taste how sweet you are when you come.' His voice is rough with need.

Oh damn. That's… I've never had that before… Everything below my ribs pulls tight.

'I'm not some…some dessert.' But my hips rock forward anyway, betraying me. Need detonates under my skin, wildfire-quick, every synapse screaming *more, now, yours* in a language older than shame.

He turns me around to face him. 'I want to make you

come on my tongue. Until you forget every damn rule you've ever made.'

'Pretty sure we burned those rules last night…' I bite my lip as he sinks to his knees in front of me, his breath hot against my stomach. 'And why are you smirking?'

This. Is. Happening.

He hooks one of my legs up, guiding it over his shoulder with one hand, the other braced on my hip. My heel rests against the flex of his back. His breath ghosts over me and I shudder.

'Hold on, baby. This is where all control goes out the window.'

His mouth hits me like a power surge, sudden voltage straight to my core. There's no finesse. Nothing but the wet, teasing lick of his tongue. I've never felt anything like it.

He devours me and I come apart like cheap lace.

'Fuck. God. Oh god.' I choke on my own breath as he drinks me in, all growling approval and worshipful greed.

The abrasive scrape of stubble sends sparks skittering up my thighs. His grip borders on cruel, welding me to his lips like he owns the space between my legs.

My hand shoots out, gripping his hair. 'Jesus. Finn…'

His groan thrums against me. The leg he's got on his shoulder is trembling. He seals his lips right there, sucking like he's trying to steal my soul through my clit.

Do I let out a tiny scream?

Yes, yes I do.

'Damn, you taste good,' he mutters against me, barely pulling back.

I can't answer. I'm panting, one hand fisted in his hair, the other bracing against the counter, trying not to collapse.

Finn flattens his tongue and strokes slow and wide against my clit until I'm keening. Heat coils deep, low, unbearable. He opens me with his thumb and goes deeper, tongue circling the way his fingers did earlier, but wetter, faster, intimate in a way that makes my eyes sting.

My grip on his hair tightens. 'Don't stop,' I gasp, already close.

Finn pulls me in until there's nowhere left to hide. I'm spread wide for him, one heel resting on his broad shoulder, chest heaving.

'Finn...' My voice breaks.

His tongue moves tighter, faster. Then he sucks again, hard and perfect. My whole body snaps. I scream again and nearly slide down the cupboard, white heat ripping through me in waves so intense that everything blurs. I'm not in my kitchen, not even in my body. I'm only need and his mouth and the endless, rolling aftershocks he won't let me outrun.

I can't speak. I can't think. My hand stays tangled in his hair. Because if I let go, I'll float straight off the planet.

Finally he pulls back and kisses the inside of my thigh, lips still wet with me. 'Good?'

I manage a breathless, stunned, 'This was... I guess I could *die* from this.'

'I hope not, you're too delicious.' He looks up at me, eyes glittering. 'But are you gonna fix the *massive* problem I woke up with?'

I'm still trying to gather what's left of my brain, but that's an offer I'm not going to refuse. 'If it bothers you *that* much...'

'Oh, it bothers me *very* much.' He kisses my knee and stands.

The shift in height is dizzying. I'm still leaning on the counter, legs wobbly. Finn saunters to his suitcase, the same one I mocked him for when he first moved in a week ago, and pulls out another condom. Of course he's stocked up, he's probably on a monthly subscription. The foil rips with a serrated whisper. I clench tight around nothing, my body remembering the shape of him, and my ribs contract as if my lungs refuse to work until he's back inside me. Not even my breath behaves anymore.

This is me now, apparently.

Finn rolls it on. 'Bend over, baby. Let me see what's been making my mornings so difficult.'

He closes the distance, fist wrapped tight around himself. Without wasting a second, he hooks an arm around my waist, pulling me back against him with a low growl of approval, then guides me forward until my elbows touch the cool stone.

'There you go.' He nudges my feet wider. One hand stays on my hip. 'Keep that pretty arse up where I need it.'

Finn swipes up and down my wetness a few times. Then he presses forward, filling me to the edge of what I can take. I bite down a whimper and try not to weep.

'Move, please. Move.' I can't bear that he's holding still and push back into him.

'Theo. Baby. I can't believe you—' his voice catches for a second, '—want this as bad as I do.' He starts to thrust slowly. 'Fuck, you take me so good.'

My eyes flutter closed and my body throbs around him. Each movement drives a sound from me I don't recognise.

'You feel that, Theo? How much I fucking want you?'

'Yes, yes!' I'm biting my wrist.

'Does my cock feel good?'

'God, yes!' I wriggle against him.

He lets out a shaky breath. 'Trying to last more than five seconds here and you're *not* helping.'

I smile between the sighs. He moves just right and keeps going, and the smile falls clean off my face on a moan. Our rhythm builds, a push and pull that keeps me between pleasure and surrender, ecstasy blazing all the way up through my veins and—

A low thump on the counter.

Elvis?

That furry menace lands in front of me and stares straight

at us, tail twitching, then meows with theatrical outrage as if he's joining a meeting we forgot to invite him to.

A jagged laugh bursts out of me. 'You have got to be joking.'

Finn's chest shakes against my back. Elvis meows again, louder this time. Positively demanding.

'We're being judged.' Finn groans, stilling inside me. 'He's got shite timing.'

I laugh, breathless. I don't know how this is my life, but it is. And I'm enjoying every moment.

'Would you like to move this meeting to my bedroom?' I ask. 'Closed door and all that.'

'Aye. Let me make you come in your bed a million times so you'll always think of me when you sleep in it.'

He gently pulls out and I turn to make the loss more bearable, catching his mouth in a kiss. My hands find his.

And I let him lead me home.

Chapter 18

Finn

The Kelpies shimmer in the pale daylight as we pass them, their steel flanks catching the weak February sun. Theo's gazing out the car window, legs crossed, one boot bouncing gently with the road's rhythm. Her profile's sharp in the dim light. Thoughtful, unreadable, and a complete knockout.

I should be focussed on the road.

We're on the M9 heading for Stirling. The sky has that weird, washed-out blue that makes it seem later than it is. It's quiet in the car. Not awkward quiet, good quiet. We're not talking. We don't need to.

She glances over. 'You keep staring.'

'Yeah, well. Your face is distracting.'

'You've seen it before.'

'Still distracting.'

She rolls her eyes, but she's fighting a smile. Which means I'm winning. I know that expression now. I know a lot of things I didn't two weeks ago. Not only the way she grips my hair when I've got my tongue on her or how she swears when she's close, the in-between bits too.

Two weeks. That's how long I've been living in Theo's flat.

Was only meant to be one, but that day came and went, and neither of us said a thing. So I just...kept waking up next to her. Feels as if I've nicked something no one said I could have.

I flick the indicator. 'We've got two and a half hours before the MacKenzie Mid-Season Mixer, so I figured...pool?'

She turns to face me. 'Are you asking me on a date, Lennox?'

'I'm asking you to publicly humiliate me in front of several pensioners at Hendry Halls so I can jerk off to the memory later.'

'Romantic.'

'I'm trying.'

'Sure.' She giggles, and something behind my breastbone gives a hard twang.

The truth is, I've been thinking about that night at the party since it happened. The way she stalked around that table, confident and smug and hot with the casual lethality of a panther cleaning blood from its claws. She wiped the floor with Scottie. I'd wanted to drag her into a dark corner right then and there. Still do.

Except now I've had her – gasping into her pillow, clenching around my fingers, making those needy little sounds I've been dreaming about – and somehow I'm worse off than before.

The want's not gone. It's fucking multiplied.

I've barely slept. I've barely eaten. I've bent her over the counter, fucked her against the door, had her legs locked around me. My thighs are wrecked. My groin's tight. My lower back has a dull, satisfied ache. I'm not even sure I can sprint right now.

And I don't give a shit. I'd rather limp onto the pitch tomorrow than miss a single sound she makes when she comes. I'm getting more hooked on her happiness than the game.

Didn't see that coming.

Rucked Up Ruse

. . .

Hendry Halls is half pub, half shrine. Signed posters of snooker legends on every wall. The old carpet holds the faint smell of battered sausage and vinegar. The table is a bit warped, but Theo leans over like there's prize money riding on it. She lines up her shot, brows pinched in concentration. Her boot nudges against mine for balance. The ball clacks clean into the corner pocket.

She straightens. 'That's four–nil.'

'I'm still finding my flow.' I'm chalking my cue like it's going to help. 'Or maybe I'm lulling you into a false sense of security.'

She laughs. 'You said that two games ago.'

'Still true. You'll never see it coming.'

She grins, smug as hell, and sips her orange fizzy juice. I made sure the pub had it. Aye, I called ahead like a sappy bastard. Worth it.

'You're not bad, for someone whose entire life is balls.' She takes a seat on one of the scuffed leather benches.

I blink at her. 'Did you seriously make a testicle joke?'

'I did. You may now retire.'

'Oh, you've changed, MacMickin.'

Her lips twist as if she's tasting something delicious and slightly illegal. 'No. I've *adapted*.'

I sit beside her, our shoulders close. The room hums with old jukebox sound and quiet commentary from a nearby table.

'You done kicking my arse, or do you need another one to really drive it home?'

Theo stretches her arms. 'I could go again. But it seems a bit unfair. Like hustling a toddler.'

'You're enjoying this way too much.'

'Perhaps a little.' Her gaze is skating over the posters.

Steve Davis. Ronnie O'Sullivan. Hendry himself. 'A pool den. Is this where you usually take girls on a date?'

I huff through my nose. 'I don't usually take anyone on dates.'

'C'mon. It can't all have been threesomes and foursomes and mindless shagging.'

I make a noise that's basically *yeah, and?*

She fixes me with that look people save for liars and politicians.

'Awright, maybe not all. But mostly. I was never the relationship guy.'

'Why not?'

I rest my cue against the bench. 'Because shagging's easier when you've got nowhere to sleep. If someone cute fancied me and had central heating? That was enough.'

'That's not all, though. Is it?'

'I had a girlfriend, once,' I say. 'Before all that, when I was fifteen. Joanna. We were together a year. First time I ever felt…safe, maybe. Until it all went to shite and I didn't have a place to land anymore. Her parents didn't want her with the homeless lad fae Easterhoose.'

Theo's face softens, but she doesn't say anything. Just gives me that silence she does. She's making space instead of trying to fill it.

'After that, I figured it was better to be the one walking away early,' I say. 'Or, better yet, not stay at all.'

'Did you ever fall in love?'

I pick at a tear in the leather seat. 'Not properly. Plenty of lust and drama. But naw. Never got to the bit with the toothbrush at mine. That stuff.'

'Do you want that stuff?' She lists her head sideways, one eyebrow curving up. 'Not everybody does.'

'Used to think I didn't. Thought I'd cock it up. But lately… I keep catching myself daydreaming about matching strawberry jammies.'

Rucked Up Ruse

Her gaze drops to her cue, but not before I catch that quick flare behind her lashes. 'That's disturbingly wholesome.'

'It is. Domesticity's corrupted me.'

She laughs again, and it's warm and real and right here between us.

'I don't want to be a prick, Theo. I don't want to be like my da. Or the lads I saw growing up who used their fists more than their mouths. I want to be better.'

She's quiet for a second. 'You already are.'

'What about you? Didn't you mention a break up in London?'

I picture some smug bastard with his hands on her, her laugh in his mouth, and something ugly coils in my chest. Jealousy, yeah. But there's pain too. That she let someone in before me. That he fucked it up so much that she's having a hard time opening up again.

She blows out a breath. 'You ever trust someone and then realise they only were with you because you made them look better? It sucks.'

'Aye. It does.'

Silence for a moment. Not heavy, just turned a notch tighter.

'Gil was more than my boyfriend,' she says eventually. 'He was my manager at the agency in London. Brilliant, older, charming. Everyone adored him. Including me.'

My shoulders hitch. 'Sounds like a puffed-up arsehole.'

'He knew how to say the right things: that I was talented, promising, amazing. He sent me flowers and took me on dates, called me first thing in the morning and late at night. Like I was exceptional and he couldn't believe his luck. And I believed him.' Her eyes are on the table now. 'Love bombing is what the kids call it nowadays. And I wasn't prepared for that.'

'You're always prepared for everything, Theo.'

'Not for a grade A narcissist as it turned out. He started

using my work. Strategy decks, campaign ideas. Stuff I stayed up all night building. He'd take my ideas, polish them with a grin, and pitch them as his.'

'And you found out.'

She nods. 'At a party. One of our biggest clients. That account was a huge deal for me. I stood next to the bar while he told the room my ideas like he'd dreamt them up in the shower. Everyone clapped and called him a genius. I just… stood there, floored.'

'What a fucking twat.'

'When I confronted him, he told me not to be dramatic. Said I was making things personal. That I was threatening his position. He made me feel like I was unstable. Even though I found out that I wasn't the first young female employee he did that to.'

The wood beneath my hand creaks. Hadn't noticed I was gripping the table.

'I escalated it, and HR got involved. He flipped it and told them I was stalking him because I was starstruck by his reputation or whatever. They didn't exactly fire me, but they let me go quietly when my contract ended. The project I built got reassigned. My name disappeared.'

She says it all calmly. But her jaw ticks once, and I know it's costing her.

'That bastard stole from you,' I say. 'And then made you feel like you were the problem. You don't happen to still have his address? Asking for an itching fist.'

'Don't be daft, Finn.'

I'm not daft, I'm raging. But I swallow it for her sake. 'You ever see him again?'

'No. And I wouldn't trust myself not to pour boiling water in his lap, so that's for the best.'

I let that hang for a second. 'So…what's it like, trying to trust me?'

Her mouth crooks. 'Probably risky, but oddly thrilling.'

Rucked Up Ruse

'I'll take that.'

She puts a hand on my cheek. 'You're a cocky menace with no off switch, but you've never made me feel small. Not once.'

I bite back the victory in my smile, but my ribs tighten anyway. 'That's only because you terrify me.'

Another laugh slips free, and her lashes dip as if she knows what that laugh does to me.

'Wanna play one more? I think I've finally figured out which end of the cue to use.'

She stands. 'You're going down so hard, Lennox.'

What can I say? I've never felt more like a winner than when I'm losing to Theo MacMickin.

And I never thought I had a type.

Turns out, I just hadn't met her yet.

We're pushing through the door of the Sin & Tonic for MacKenzie's Mid-Season Mixer after the Six Nations kick-off viewing party. A wall of noise hits first: boozy chatter, the tinny echo of a sports highlights reel from the TV on the wall, and glasses clinking against wooden tables. MacKenzie Sporting banners hang from every available surface, blue and white with their mountain logo gleaming under the pub lights. The match finished twenty minutes ago – Scotland squeaked a win – and now the business begins.

I guide Theo through the throng with a hand where her back curves in. Her spine straightens under my touch. Not pulling away, but aware we're being watched.

'There they are.' Charlie waves from a booth, Brodie beside her. Still a brooding dick, but a lot less so with her around. He'll never be a ray of sunshine, but he's become a real mate.

Across the room, Scottie merely lifts his chin in acknowledgement. He's wedged into a corner with Connor, who's mid-story, arms flying. But Scottie's gaze is fixed on the other side of the bar, where Ava is standing with her boyfriend Nevin. He has a possessive arm clamped around her waist while she stares at her shoes. Scottie's glaring at Nevin as if he's imagining him six feet under.

We reach the booth. Brodie grunts a hello, and Charlie's eyes flick between me and Theo, her smile curling as if she's five steps ahead.

'Glad you could make it. MacKenzie wants a word. Let's keep the golden couple on show.'

The MacKenzie CEO – Gordon something, grey suit, shiny watch – catches my eye from the bar and lifts his drink. I nod back, feeling Theo move beside me.

'We're being watched.' She elbows me discreetly. 'Behave.'

'Never.' I catch her wrist before she moves away. 'Kiss for luck?'

Her eyes widen fractionally. She rises on tiptoe and presses her lips to mine, quick but firm. A kiss designed for the public, yet real enough to leave a mark. I feel eyes on us, curious and calculating. But mostly I feel my heart thumping so loudly it drowns out the room.

'Alright, Romeo,' Charlie interrupts. 'Photos now, canoodling later.'

I follow her through the crowd, catching snippets of conversations as we go. Coach Wallace is nursing a coke in the corner, nodding solemnly at Jamie.

Gordon MacKenzie claps me on the shoulder when I reach him. 'Lennox! Good to see you settling down, lad.' His eyes sweep over Theo, assessing.

I smile through gritted teeth. 'She's something else.'

'Listen, lad. We've all sown our wild oats, some of us more thoroughly than others. But two at once?' MacKenzie whistles through his teeth, low and slow. 'That's a hell of a stat. Still, best to stick with one now. A good lass by your side, the right kind of headlines… That sort of taming does wonders for a man's reputation and our brand. We're a family company, after all.'

His tone's pissing me off.

'Smile, boys.' Charlie positions me next to Brodie and the kit display before I can tell MacKenzie where to shove his family values.

I throw my arm around Brodie's shoulder. 'How's it feel to be a nice guy, eh?'

He gives a low, grudging sound. 'Weird. How does it feel to finally grow up?'

'Even weirder.'

Theo's fringe falls across her forehead as she concentrates. 'Perfect. You look respectable, Lennox.'

'Blasphemy.'

She winks at me.

And I know with gut-punching, balls-kicking clarity that I'd trade every single wild oat I've sown to be the man she comes home to.

Three hours, three Irn Brus, and a dozen smiling photo ops later, the pub's lost its buzz. Most of the crowd has trickled out.

We're still at the same booth, but the circle's thinned. Jamie's long gone, muttering something about protein and priorities. Scottie ducked out halfway through and never came back. Now it's just me, Theo, Brodie, and Charlie. She's perched sideways, back against the wall, one boot on the seat. Theo's curled beside me, half-leaning, eyes soft with the fatigue that comes after too much noise.

Next to Charlie, Brodie lounges with one arm draped along the back of their bench, fingers absentmindedly tracing slow circles against her jacket. He's relaxed in that way only people in love seem to master. He knows where he belongs. Charlie leans into it. Doesn't even seem to notice she's doing it. I do. And I'm not proud of the thought that hits me next. A quiet ache. That half-conscious yearning for something settled and real.

I want this with Theo.

We said we'd keep this thing going till May. Ride it out through the season and reassess. See where we stand. But I already know where I stand. Right fucking here. With her. Only, I've no idea if she's standing anywhere near me. Or if she's already half-packed, ready to bolt the second the clock runs out.

Charlie sips her gin and sets it down with exaggerated precision. Her lips are pressed together in a tight smile that keeps threatening to split into a wide grin.

She can't be pregnant, she's drinking gin. So that's not it.

'I've got news. Big news,' she finally admits. 'Can't say yet. Don't want to tempt fate. Let's just say all this relationship spin might've worked better than planned. A lot better.'

Theo narrows her eyes. 'Better how?'

'Oh, you'll see.' Charlie smile gets broader.

I tip my chair slightly. 'That's ominous.'

'No. It's promising,' she says. 'Don't worry, I'll fill you in as soon as the timing's right.'

'You're such a tease,' Theo says dryly.

Charlie shrugs, but she's clearly fit to burst. 'I'm only saying that your public snogs might've tipped things in our favour. That's all.'

I stare Theo down like she's the one who invented kissing. 'We are extremely snog-forward. That's not a bad thing.'

Charlie twists her glass slowly between her fingers, still grinning. 'It's not. Not at all.'

Brodie leans back, his arm behind her. 'You done being cryptic, or should we get a translator?'

'Dance with me, and I might cave.' She nudges him with her knee.

He sighs, stands, and holds out a hand. 'Awright, Champ.

But only because I don't want to hear Finn try to be seductive again.'

They disappear toward a slow song coming through the speakers. Something with a saxophone and too much reverb.

Theo watches them go and lets out a yawn that stretches through her whole body. 'I need my bed.'

'Is that code for "Please eat my pussy again, Finn, *please please please*"?'

'That's not how I sound.' Her laugh's low and throaty. 'But now I'm reconsidering my definition of tired.'

I drag my nose along the curve of her ear, catching the sweet scent of her skin. 'Your boiler's still being a temperamental bastard, aye? My place is two minutes from here. Come crash at mine. I'll heat you up properly.'

She eyes me, weighing it. 'But I have to check on Elvis early tomorrow morning. He's got heaps of food and three hot water bottles, but…'

'…he's your spoilt little prince of hell,' I finish. 'Nae bother. We'll set an alarm. You can ride my face first thing, then feed your cat. Two pussies, one happy morning.'

'If there's one thing I'll be begging for, Lennox,' she says with that sparkle in her eyes, 'it's that you stop making group sex jokes.'

Chapter 19

Theo

I wake up with my face mushed into warm skin, my arm flung across a broad chest. My leg is hooked over his, my body wrapped around him like he's an extra-large human comfort pillow.

The disorientation lasts precisely three seconds.

Then I remember. Finn's flat. Last night.

He's sprawled on his back, the pillow above his head, one arm tucked beneath mine. Even asleep, there's an intensity about him that makes the room seem fuller.

My eyes adjust to the half-light filtering through a bent blind.

Oh yeah, I'm in Finn Lennox's actual bedroom.

I attempt a reconnaissance mission without disturbing him. The wall behind his bed is painted matte black – bold choice, but unsurprising considering his hair – with a framed 90s Chicago Bulls jersey mounted in the centre. Signed by Rodman and likely worth more than my monthly mortgage payment.

An impressive collection of trainers lines the wall opposite, each pair squeaky clean and arranged by colour. His rugby kit occupies a corner.

Rucked Up Ruse

The sheets beneath me are crisp linen. No satin or silk or anything that screams 'I seduce ladies here on the reg'. They smell of fabric softener and him – that addictive combination.

A weighted blanket sits folded at the foot of the bed. For his nightmares? That night on the sofa, when his panic unlatched something between us, I stayed because I couldn't leave. That night was the start of it, and I've been catching up ever since. I fell bit by bit and didn't feel the drop until now.

My gaze drifts, searching for something to hold on to.

No photos or plants. No pieces of himself or his past on display. Two full bookshelves, though. I squint to make out titles. Looks like sports autobiographies, yes, but also fantasy paperbacks with sprayed edges.

I'm still tracing the way his breath moves under my cheek when his phone's alarm blares, a jarring electronic jingle that shatters the quiet.

Finn groans, burying his face in the pillow as he fumbles for the snooze button. 'Hngh. Five more minutes.'

'No rest for the wicked.'

He pulls me closer and finds the curve of my waist. 'Morning, List Girl.'

'Morning, Rugby God.'

'Don't call me that.' He presses his nose into my hair. 'It's weird.'

'You are weird.'

He grins, his breath hot against my ear. 'But you like it.'

'Maybe.'

'And I like you here. In my bed, in my shirt, with your hair all witchy.'

'It's not witchy!' I don't argue further, mostly because I'm suddenly too aware of the way we're wound into each other and how lovely that feels. I let my eyes roam again.

'You cataloguing my possessions?' His voice is sleep-rough and amused.

'I'm merely assessing the environment. Didn't really get the chance last night.'

'And what's your assessment?' His mouth curls upward.

'That you're surprisingly tidy for someone who oozes so much chaos.'

He draws his fingertips up my back along my spine. 'Chaos has its place in the world.'

'And that place is everywhere except your bedroom?'

'This room is for sleeping.' He opens one eye, a startling shade of sky blue in the dim light. 'Usually.'

'Oi! We *did* sleep.'

'Aye, eventually.' There's that smug little smirk in his voice again.

I should move. Should peel myself away from him and remember all the reasons why falling for Finn Lennox is career suicide and emotional roulette and a bad, bad idea.

Well. Too damn late. I've already started rewriting the calendar. May's not an end anymore. So I burrow closer. Because there's nowhere else I want to be.

His thigh is snug between mine, scratchy hair against my calf. He does that thing again where he drags the tip of his nose along my neck.

'You smell like my sheets now,' he murmurs.

'And you smell like last night.'

'Mhm. That was a good one.' Finn nuzzles closer, arm banding around my middle. He reaches under the hem of the shirt I'm wearing – his, obviously – and rests his palm against my belly. As if he's checking I'm still there.

This is nice.

So, so nice.

My foot finds his under the duvet and we toe-wrestle lazily until he cheats and traps mine between both of his.

The alarm rings again.

Finn sighs, reluctantly reaching for his phone to silence it. 'We have to feed your wee ginger demon.'

'I know.' I ease out from his arms, sit up, and push my hair back like I'm about to ask a serious question. 'But... Didn't you say something about one morning, two pussies?'

Yeah, I went there. This is what has become of me, courtesy of Finlay Lennox.

'Aye.' He beams as he pulls me up. 'And one busy tongue.'

By the time I've come twice and am finally scraping tuna into Elvis's bowl, my cat's side-eying me as if I've committed high treason.

'It was twelve hours. You had three hot water bottles.'

He sniffs, circles once, then grudgingly eats, showing me his little bum.

Finn leans in the doorway, hands in the pockets of his jeans, hoodie still creased from the car. His hair's damp from the drizzle, and there's a faint smear of toothpaste on his collar.

'Is he always this dramatic?' Finn asks.

'He's used to being the only man in my life. You're encroaching on his turf.'

'Tough shit. I've got better arms.'

I roll my eyes, but yeah. He's not wrong.

Finn moves to the cupboard as if he's lived here for years and reaches for the tin behind the oats without needing to check. Then he measures the leaves with precision, fills the kettle, and wipes yesterday's tea ring off the counter with the hem of his sleeve.

'You've memorised my kitchen.'

'Not hard. You've got seven things in here.'

He moves through my flat with the same economy he carries on the pitch. As if he's mapped every corner already.

I sit first on the couch, and he joins me without comment, stretching his legs until they press against the opposite armrest. His sock has a hole at the toe. I see it. He doesn't bother to hide it.

We folded the sofa bed away ages ago. He's stayed in my bed since that morning and hasn't had a single nightmare.

'This isn't the worst place I've slept,' he says calmly.

'I know.' My heart aches when I think about what happened to him when he was little more than a boy.

It's only been a few weeks, but I spent every free moment thinking about, writing posts for, or being with Finn. I don't need months to see what's going on here.

This is special.

And…I want him to have a home. With me and Elvis.

Rain beats against the glass with quiet insistence, and the radiator ticks once. Finn's knee presses against mine and stays there. He belongs here. As though he's always been part of the furniture, the cat, the mugs. My life.

I should say something and be bold enough to ask what happens after the last game in May. Should tell him I don't want this to end. But the words lodge behind my teeth like a popcorn kernel. Irritating and impossible to spit out without making a scene. If I say it, I can't unsay it. And if he doesn't say it back… Well. Then we're both fucked, and not in the good way.

It would break my heart.

So I don't.

He doesn't either.

But it's right here between us.

He rests his hand low on my thigh, fingers curling against the seam of my jeans. His touch makes it hard to remember why we ever called this pretend. I press my heel against his shin just to feel him.

Then my phone buzzes on the coffee table. I groan and grab it. Text from Charlie:

Rucked Up Ruse

> Hope you're making the most of your fake love fest. Come to the office asap. We've got a game-changer!!

She used exclamation marks, plural. Charlie never uses exclamation marks.

Finn leans over to read it. He stills, jaw working through something unsaid. 'You think it's about us?'

'It's definitely something,' I say, already standing. I drain my mug.

Finn sets his down beside mine. 'Let's go find out.'

The short drive to Elite Edge takes us through the crawl of Edinburgh's morning rush. Rain patters against the windshield, blurring the grand Georgian townhouses into a watercolour painting of grey stone.

Finn finds my hand on the gearstick and shoots me a sideways look. 'You're overthinking again.'

I keep my eyes on the car ahead. 'It's my speciality.'

'I know. Your forehead gets this little crease right here.' He taps between my eyebrows.

I hate how he's so observant and smooth my expression. 'No, it doesn't.'

'It does. And it's cute.'

Fifteen minutes later, I park my car behind the old factory now co-working space.

The rain's stopped, leaving the streets slick and gleaming under a bruised sky. The air smells of wet stone and exhaust fumes.

Auld Reekie.

Our floor is buzzing with mid-morning energy as we step off the lift. Edinburgh's skyline looms beyond the windows, jagged rooftops and moody clouds threatening rain again. February isn't Scotland's prettiest month.

Charlie's perched on her desk, heels clicking rhythmically against the filing cabinet, phone clutched in her hand as if it's a winning lottery ticket.

'You will not believe this.' She launches herself at us for a group hug.

Finn stiffens for a fraction of a second, then relaxes into it.

'It's better than any of us could've dreamt. Got the confirmation this morning. Time to make it official.'

Charlie is not a hugger. So whatever this is, it's huge.

'Sit.' She flaps a hand at the client chairs. 'Before I combust on the spot.'

Finn slouches beside me, knee brushing mine. I focus on the stray thread unravelling from his hoodie sleeve instead of the way his thumb traces circles on my thigh. Having Finn Lennox in my workplace is a bit like bringing a tiger to a tea party. A very hot, cuddly, welcome tiger.

It's wild how much I'm feeling this. Him, the proximity, the low current of whatever this is between us. I didn't expect to let anyone in ever again, least of all this hot mess of a flanker. But I can't stop it. I can't stop what breaks loose inside when he touches me, or the way my pulse picks up every time he's near. The continuous drip of something that might be love.

That word.

Big and heavy and scary.

But yeah. There's a possibility that I might be in love with Finn Lennox.

I should be focussed on what Charlie's about to say. I should have a guess, at least a whiff of a hint. I'm her assistant, for fuck's sake. But I've got nothing. No memo, no whisper, no clue. And I don't know whether to laugh or panic.

'Spill it, boss,' I say. 'You're making me a smidge nervous.'

Rucked Up Ruse

Charlie beams and slams a thin folder onto the desk. 'Tell me you like croissants, because you're moving to France. RC Marseille-Provence wants you, Finn. As in right now, mid-season. They've made an offer.'

The office is suddenly airless. I grip the edge of my chair, nails digging into the faux leather.

Finn blinks rapidly, his mouth slightly open. 'Marseille? A French club?'

'Oui, a French club!' Her eyes go wide with glee.

My brain whirs, trying to process this bombshell.

France. Finn in France.

The words refuse to connect properly, like mismatched puzzle pieces.

Marseille. France. As in, *not here*.

My mind races, piecing together the cryptic calendar entries, the hushed phone calls Charlie had taken over the past few weeks.

'How did I not hear about this?' The question spills out before I can filter it. 'Were those the appointments with C. Dreyfus?'

Charlie's smile falters slightly. She tucks a strand of hair behind her ear. 'I'm so sorry. I couldn't say anything until it was official. Super top secret, need-to-know basis and all that jazz.'

'Right.' I nod mechanically.

Logically, I get it. She couldn't tell me. I'm Elite Edge's social media manager and assistant. Not privy to high-level negotiations. Still, a microscopic needle of hurt pricks deep in my chest.

Finn's eyes dart between us, his Adam's apple bobbing as he swallows. 'Hold on. I'm missing something here. Why now? Why me?'

Charlie perches on the desk and crosses her ankles. 'Their star flanker tore a ligament in his knee. Season-ending injury. French Top fourteen clubs can sign players outside the transfer window under "joker médical" rules. Essentially an injury replacement.'

'And they want…me?'

'They need a hard-hitting, high-profile flanker who can make an immediate impact,' Charlie continues. 'Someone who draws press attention both on and off the pitch. They're known for taking on…less disciplined players.'

I watch his profile, the slight furrow between his brows deepening. His knee has stopped its casual brush against mine. Now it's bobbing.

'Their sporting director loved our rebrand strategy.' Charlie grins, wickedly pleased with herself. 'The redemption narrative we've been crafting worked like a charm.'

The muscle under his ear twitches. Locked down, but not fast enough.

Charlie doesn't seem to notice his reaction. 'Think about it. You're perfect: young, talented. There's already media buzz swirling around you. An affordable risk with a high PR upside.' She's on a roll and oblivious to the two stiff people sitting in front of her. 'The French club sees commercial potential in you.'

'Right. Commercial potential.' He stirs in his seat. The thread on his sleeve has unravelled further, and he tugs at it absently.

'Most Top fourteen players are already under contract,' Charlie explains. 'But the pressure from Lord Dalcrieff, whose fiancée you…'

'… slept with,' Finn finishes flatly.

Charlie winces. 'Yes. That situation makes this a perfect escape hatch. If you want it.'

A bitter tide surges in my stomach. *Escape hatch.* The phrase echoes in my head. My mind is a swirling vortex of what-ifs and oh-gods. France. He'd be in fucking *France*. For good.

'When would this happen?' I ask.

Rucked Up Ruse

'Soon,' Charlie replies. 'They want him in Marseille by next week.'

Next week. Two syllables, frostbite-sharp, carving space between my ribs.

'What about my current contract with the Rebels?' Finn asks.

'I wanted to talk to you first before I poke that particular bear.' Charlie says. 'I'm sure they'd like to keep you, but considering what's been going on, they might also be open to it. I could get it done.'

Finn rubs his palm across his jaw, the scratch of stubble audible in the quiet room. 'I see.'

'The financial package is impressive.' She pushes the folder toward him. '200,000 pounds gross per year; 60,000 pounds signing bonus; 20,000 pounds per year in image rights and sponsorship. Fully covered relocation, housing, French-language coaching. Plus, Marseille in spring is lovely. Sunshine, Mediterranean lifestyle…'

I stare at a small water stain on the ceiling, trying to ignore the emptiness expanding in my chest. The Mediterranean is over a thousand miles from Edinburgh.

'And what about—' Finn starts, then stops abruptly.

Yeah. What about us?

Those unsaid words are like a tripwire between us, and we're both too terrified to set it off.

Charlie glances at us. 'This is a lot to take in. But career-wise, Finn, this is a golden ticket. The board at RC Marseille-Provence meets early next week. They want an answer in three days, so Monday.'

'Three days?' His tone fractures.

'You know how it is,' Charlie says. 'They need to move quickly, since it's mid-season.'

I force myself to breathe normally, even as panic bubbles beneath my skin. Three days. One weekend. Seventy-two hours to process that the man who's somehow become central to my existence with lightning speed, the only man who ever made me feel complete and myself, might drop out of my world just as fast.

This is the chance of a lifetime.

'I need to think,' Finn says, standing abruptly. His chair squeaks against the floor.

'Of course,' Charlie nods. 'Take the contract details with you. Review the terms.' Then she turns to me, eyes gleaming with pride. 'Our first international contract! We did it, Theo!'

'Our? We?'

'Yeah. This wouldn't have happened without you. Nothing would.' Now she grins like the cat that got the cream. 'How does a full partnership sound to you?'

Chapter 20

Finn

The lift is one of those old cage ones with steel bars and mirrors scratched at the corners. We step in without speaking. Theo hits the button, then wraps her arms around the folder. She stands beside me but feels miles away. The doors clank shut, and the sound echoes up my spine.

France.

What does that even mean?

New kit, new flat, new language I don't speak. A new team that doesn't know me, doesn't owe me anything. Starting over. Again.

Maybe I should be buzzing, posting a smug wee statement online. But all I can think is: it's not here.

It's not *her*.

Theo's reflection is a blur in the mirror. Straight shoulders, lips drawn tight and her chin slightly up. I don't know if she's furious or somewhere I can't reach. Probably both.

I hear her breathing, though. Short, even inhales, like she's counting them. I want to say something to fill the silence, or maybe just to hear my own voice, make sure I still have one. But I don't trust my mouth. It's full of gravel. My back's against the bars. I shift, and the lift groans like it doesn't want to move.

Theo doesn't look at me.

If I reach for her now, and she pulls away, I don't know what I'll do.

I scan the floor. There's a bit of grit in the corner, a greasy thumbprint on the button panel. Her perfume's faint but there. It winds itself into my centre, tighter with every breath, until I feel it in my teeth.

'That was a surprise if ever there was one.' It comes out a lot lighter than I feel.

'You should do it.' She sounds soft and nearly sincere. But it cleaves right through me.

'What?' My throat clamps down, throttling the syllables. 'Marseille?'

She nods once, without turning her face my way. 'Yes. Charlie's right. This is a huge deal. For you, obviously. But also for Elite Edge.'

Ah. There it is.

'So that's what this is about.' I try for a dismissive laugh, but my throat is too dry. 'The agency.'

Of course. The agency comes first. Her job always does. And I get it, she's brilliant. She deserves a full partnership and all the success she can get. More than a fuck-up with pink hair and a questionable past.

She fidgets beside me but still doesn't look at me. That hurts more than it should. My body's gone hypersensitive, everything's turned up too high. The stale lift air, the hum of the lights, the hiss of the track as we sink lower.

'I'm not saying it's not personal,' she murmurs. 'But that's… It's a fantastic opportunity.' Her mouth opens like she might say something real – then shuts with a breath through her nose.

I glance sideways. Whatever she's holding in, it's tearing

through her. Pale cheeks, lips pinched, a sheen on her brow like she's burning up from the inside.

'Is that the PR line or yours, Theo?'

The pause is a brick to the sternum. Her knuckles tighten on the folder, and the silence rings like a fire alarm, loud enough to rattle my skull. I press the back of my head to the steel.

She still doesn't answer.

'What about…us?' I ask.

Now her gaze shoots my way. Brief, sharp, and agonised. For a second, her throat works like she might speak, but nothing comes. Her whole body's tense, a breath held too long.

I shift towards her – just enough for my arm to brush hers. 'Theo, if I… Maybe I could…or you…' I don't finish it. My tongue's too thick.

I can fucking *see* her pushing it all down.

Breaks my heart.

'Don't make this harder than it has to be.' She sounds as if she's angry at herself for almost hoping. 'I will *not* stand in the way of your success. And I don't think you'd want to stand in mine. This was only ever temporary, Finn. Until May.'

I let the words chew through me. I could beg and say the words. Fight to stay. But I've done that before. I've *begged* to be kept, knocked on that door for hours until my knuckles bled.

I can't do it again.

And it feels like pulling a knife out of my own chest.

'You ever think,' I say, barely above the creak of the lift, 'how different it could be if timing didn't fuck everything?' She goes still beside me, and I push on a little. 'If things were…later. Or earlier. Or…'

Nothing from her but breath. One sharp inhale. 'Finn. No.'

It shuts the thought down, and my chest cracks open. Quietly. Like it always does.

She adjusts her grip, arms crossed tighter now, as if she can hold it all in by force. 'Try to see it this way: we did it. We didn't just save your career, we made it shine. You're going to get the recognition you deserve. You deserve the spotlight. Everything this will give you. You deserve this more than anyone.' Her breath falters on the final syllable.

I nod because I can't do anything else. If I open my mouth now, I don't know what'll come out. A laugh, a scream.

Two floors down, two hundred feet deeper in the pit.

She's already done with me. This is her goodbye. Wrapped in a bow, polished and polite.

I watch her hands instead of her face. I remember sucking those fingers into my mouth. I remember her thighs clenching around my hips. I remember us in her kitchen. Theo singing along to that daft advert jingle, making that green frog drink. I remember her laugh.

It felt like something we'd keep. Like we had time.

I thought I was more than a job. That we were more than the plan. But perhaps that was just me, dreaming on her time. I was never a real choice. Just the right problem at the right time. Something to fix. And a good time along the way.

I swallow, but it catches halfway. My chest is too tight to breathe right. Every inhale is shallow and wrong, pulled through a straw. I stare at the mirror above the panel. We're reflected side by side, close but not touching.

I want to say, *Don't do this. Just ask me. I'll drop the contract. I'll torch the deal. I'll stay. Fuck, I'll stay forever.*

But if she won't ask, and I can't offer… Then maybe that's the answer. Maybe we were never meant to survive the real world. She's giving me the out. That's what this is. A clean break wrapped in logic and ambition, so she doesn't have to admit she's scared too. Scared I'll fuck it all up. Scared she'll choose me and regret it. And she'd probably be right.

Rucked Up Ruse

Or she thinks I've already chosen. The money, the spotlight. As though that's what matters most. As if I'd leave and forget her the minute I hit French soil.

I don't blame her entirely. Because that's what the old me would've done. I'm not that Finn anymore, and she should fucking know that.

But if I say it first, if I offer everything and she still tells me to go and sends me away – I won't survive it. Not again. Not when it's her.

I already tried, and she didn't catch it. The pressure in my chest breaks like a hairline crack spidering across glass. My hands drop to my sides, and I stare straight ahead.

I'm not worth keeping.

She straightens, blinking hard as if the light's too bright. I count the seconds till the ground floor.

Six.

Five.

Four.

I'm not enough.

Three.

I never was.

Two.

I never will be.

The lift slows and shudders to a stop, but I don't move. Not while she's still beside me. I try to speak, but there's too much behind it.

The doors part. Cool air hits my face. Theo doesn't move. She's still got the folder locked to her chest. Her eyes stay on the floor.

'Finn.' Her whisper slices through me.

But it's not enough to stop me. I step out and walk. I have to get… I have to…

The paper cuts into my palm where I've folded the edge of the offer. Each step forward burns hotter than it should. My spine's damp, and the back of my shirt sticks.

No footsteps, no sound from the lift. I keep waiting for something. Her voice behind me, sharp or soft, anything.

But there's nothing. Just the foyer stretching out.

This isn't the version where she runs from me. This is the crueller version, where she stays inside and simply lets me go. Where I walk away, tearing at the seams, waiting for her to shout my name. And she doesn't make a sound.

Bad timing. Two broken people.

This was never going to have a happy ending.

I want to turn back. God, I want to. I want one more glimpse of her, standing there, *not* letting go.

I can't.

It's not that I don't want to. It's that I'm too fucking scared she won't be looking at me. Or worse: that I see in her eyes that this was never as real for her as it was for me.

Then the doors close.

Chapter 21

Theo

'Partner! Your cake finally arrived.' Charlie shoves a box into my hands. 'I had them use the good photo. The one you actually smile in.'

It's a Saturday, and we're in the office because that's where we belong. And because yesterday happened, and I can't be in my flat with all that silence and Finn's absence.

I tip the box open. It's a proper cake. A full-on, marzipan-heavy, cream-filled monstrosity. And on top of it, printed on a sheet of edible paper, is my own face. Smiling. Professional. Unbothered.

Lies. All of it.

'Oh. For me?' I barely recognise my voice; it's miles from how I feel.

'Hell yeah for you!' She's radiating enough energy to power the entire building. 'You did it, Theo. The firm's yours as much as it is mine now. The hours, your loyalty and brilliance... And what you pulled off with Finn...' She shakes her head, beaming. 'You didn't just rebrand him. You gave him the chance of a lifetime.'

'Thanks, Charlie. It means a lot.'

It does. It truly, madly, deeply does. This was the dream

and the whole bloody point. Proof that I could rebuild, that I'm worth more than my last colossal fuck-up. But right now, it feels like a consolation prize. A shiny distraction from the gaping hole Finn Lennox left.

She frowns as she reads my expression. 'Marseille is a big deal. You know that, right?'

My stomach coils, and I set the cake on my desk with meticulous care, making sure it's perfectly aligned with the edge. One small thing I can control in this swirling emotional apocalypse.

'Aye, it's a fantastic opportunity for him.' I say the correct words, use the professional phrasing. And part of me means it. The other part wants to scream.

This is a massive win for her agency. *Our* agency, I mean.

'Partners? I feel it requires a handshake.' Charlie extends a hand, a wide smile lighting up her face.

I take it with a firm grip. 'Partners,' I repeat, the word echoing in the hush that follows.

It should feel like a victory. It should feel like everything I've been working towards.

'Go on, Theo! Cut your cute face so we can eat it.'

The smiling sugar-woman on the cake looks so put-together and so pleased with herself. This is the win. This is everything I've worked for since London, the proof I'm more than a pushover and someone's gullible lackey. It's concrete and real and comes with a contract.

But all I see is the lift doors closing on Finn's back. The rigid set of his shoulders and how he didn't turn back, not even for a glimpse.

I did that. I let him think he was just a job. Because it was easier than admitting he had become everything else.

I couldn't ask him to stay. If he'd said no, if I'd seen it in his face, I wouldn't have recovered. So I told myself that he was always leaving.

But the truth is, I was terrified.

Rucked Up Ruse

Terrified he'd look at me and hesitate. That I'd say *Do you want to stay?*, and he'd go anyway. That I'd splinter in front of him, and he'd watch it happen.

Or worse, that he'd stay only for my sake. That he'd say no to Marseille and mean it at the time… But then the resentment would creep in. Every time things got hard, he'd remember the offer he turned down. And he'd blame me. I couldn't risk that. Never in a thousand years would I dream of standing in his way, of having him stay only to wish he hadn't.

So I stayed silent and gave him the out.

My face stares back at me, a sugary caricature. Icing Theo is far more composed than the real one currently trying not to crumble into a million tiny, heartbroken pieces. Feels good, getting to stab her. I pick up the knife. The plastic handle is cool and smooth in my palm as I press the blade into the corner of my own printed eye.

I hand Charlie a slice and take one for myself. My smile feels brittle.

'Stop pulling that kicked-puppy face. You deserve it, and you know it,' Charlie insists. 'You went above and beyond. Even with the whole Finn situation. You handled that beautifully. A total pro.'

Yeah, if total pro means letting him eat me out like a trifle dish morning, noon, and night.

'It was…a unique challenge.' My tone is a little too tight. She has no idea what happened, and I intend to keep it that way.

'Understatement of the century.' She grabs a napkin to wipe a stray smudge of cake from her chin. 'But seriously, Theo, you've been a rock. For me, for the agency, for everyone.'

I stare at the blinking cursor. A tiny, rhythmic, relentless pulse.

On. Off. On. Off.

Like a heart that beats mechanically, only because it has to. A pulse without a purpose.

My key sticks in the lock as it always does. I jiggle it twice, hard left, then gentle right. The door swings open.

'Elvis, I'm home.'

I drop my purse on the floor. The thud echoes through the flat, too loud in the sudden silence. Even the air feels different, thinner somehow.

I step into the living room and freeze. His suitcase is gone, his hoodie is missing from the arm of the chair. The corner where his bag sat is just a corner again. The rugby boots, which had taken up permanent residence by the radiator, have disappeared.

It's like he was never here at all.

His absence hits me physically, a sharp jab straight to my solar plexus. I press my palm against my sternum to ease the pressure.

Elvis appears from the bedroom, tail swishing with agitation. He yowls – a long, accusatory sound.

'I know, he's gone.'

My cat stalks toward me, eyes narrowed judgementally.

'This was always going to happen.'

Elvis meows again, circling my ankles once before sitting directly in my path, demanding answers I don't have.

'It was a business arrangement that got complicated. He got a better offer, and he's not one to turn that down. I'm not the one to stop him. It was just…bad timing. This happens quite often between can openers, you know?'

I move to the kitchen on autopilot, flicking on lights as I go. The brightness feels offensive, exposing Finn's absence in my flat with merciless clarity.

There's a note on the counter next to my spare set of keys, a single sheet of paper folded in half. I open it and recognise his handwriting. Blocky capitals, pressed hard into the page:

Thanks for everything. I mean it. F.

Six words is all I get. Six generic, meaningless words that could have been written to anyone – his physio, his taxi driver, his barber. I read the words again, searching for a subtext that isn't there. It's polite and final. He meant the successful rebrand, the damage control. Everything except me.

And Just 'F', not even a full 'Finn'. An initial, a sign-off.

The end.

I crease the paper's edge as I fold it again, smaller and smaller until it's just a tight square of nothing. I yank open the drawer where I keep takeaway menus, batteries, and rubber bands, and tuck it inside.

This hurts so much more than Gil. That betrayal was a slow poison, a theft of my work and my trust, the gradual deconstruction of my confidence. Losing Finn is the brutal amputation of something much more vital, and I still feel the phantom limb of him everywhere.

'He didn't even say goodbye properly,' I tell Elvis, who's watching from his perch on the counter. 'Just walked out of that lift.'

My cat yawns, unimpressed.

'I'm fine,' I insist, reaching for the kettle. 'This is fine. It's actually perfect. Clean break. No mess.'

The water splashes against the metal interior. I set it on its base with too much force and click the handle.

'We made him marketable again. He got Marseille, and I got a partnership. Everybody wins.'

Except I'm the one standing in a too-quiet flat with a chest that won't stop hurting, discussing my love life with my cat.

Elvis lets out another offended yowl, a sound with teeth in it.

'What? It's true.' I grab a mug from the cupboard. The one with the glittery rainbow. The one Finn always used because he said it matched his 'aesthetic'.

I shove it back and grab another.

'Marseille is bigger than anything we could've possibly imagined when we started. It's what he needs at this point in his career, and, as I said, I won't get in his way.' The words catch, but I push through.

We were a means to an end. A glorious, temporary, hot means to an end. I should be grateful for the memories, for the sex, for the way he made me laugh until my stomach ached. Made me scream until I had no air. Me. I've never screamed for anything in my life.

But gratitude feels like swallowing sand.

I can't cope with the loss. The before-and-after of him splits my life into two unequal halves.

Before Finn, sex was fine. Enjoyable enough, in the way a holiday you can't quite remember is still technically a holiday. I'd been with a handful of men before, and none of them were cruel or careless. They were decent and kind. Even Gil. But it always felt like something I had to manage. My expectations, their egos, the disappointment when it didn't really land. It was mostly fun, but also functional.

And then Finn turned everything on its head and changed the rules of the game for fucking ever.

He made sex feel like electricity and softness and something close to worship. I'd never been watched like that, never been handled like I was the whole point. He listened, adjusted, and watched me come apart with a quiet focus that made it impossible to hide. And I couldn't get enough.

I'd never had sex that left me undone hours later. Never

Rucked Up Ruse

walked into a meeting still aching, still reeling, still clenching around the echo of him. He was possessive. Not in a way that claimed me, but in a way that asked if I knew I could be claimed. And I let him.

Elvis flicks his tail dismissively.

'At least I'm not the one who spent a day sulking under the bed because he brought me the wrong flavour of Dreamies.'

The kettle clicks off. I pour water over a tea bag I don't remember selecting. Watch as the colour bleeds outward, turning the water a deep amber.

My entire life feels wrong and there's no scented candle to make it okay. It's too quiet, clean, and empty. Too much like before, when I was licking my wounds – except much worse because now I know what I'm missing.

What I've been missing all my life.

I miss *him*. Not the sex or the banter. Him, in all his chaotic, unfiltered glory. He never tiptoed around my edges. He barged in, filled the place with life, and made it feel like a home instead of a hole to hide in. His presence made my tightly-wound world less controlled, but also less lonely.

Pressure builds behind my breastbone again, a knotted mass of unshed tears and unspoken words. It needs to go somewhere. I turn to the bookshelf, a chaotic jumble of genres and sizes. If I can't fix the gaping wound in my heart, I can at least organise something.

I ditch the tea and move to the shelf instead.

'Red goes here,' I mutter, pulling books from shelves and stacking them on the floor. 'Then orange, yellow, green…'

Elvis watches from the sofa as I sort novels by their spines. The mindless task is supposed to soothe me. I sit back on my heels, surrounded by piles of books that suddenly mean nothing to me.

'What am I doing?' I ask Elvis, who blinks once, deeply

unfazed by the question and my general existence outside of serving him food and giving him belly rubs on demand.

I pick up my phone, Instagram is still open, and I'm greeted by a wall of red hearts. Notifications I haven't cleared. Comments. Stories. A flood of hearts and fire emojis and little gifs of cartoon couples kissing. One photo in particular – me in Finn's lap, both of us in full, unguarded smiles– is still getting likes. Comments.

So cute!! Obsessed with these two. Can't wait for the wedding! 🥺

The thought strikes without warning, a snap behind my eyes and the sick lurch of my stomach catching up a second later.

Fuck. Fuck!

Our fake relationship hasn't ended.

Not publicly. Not for the cameras or the fans or the sponsors. As far as the world knows, Finlay Lennox and Theodora MacMickin are still very much together, still Edinburgh's favourite sporty couple du jour.

The thought is a cruel joke. One last piece of shrapnel lodged deep where no one can see.

Our contract isn't up, our story not over. I'm still his fake girlfriend. I should be drafting a press release, a gushing social media post about being a supportive partner in his move to France. Long distance love and all that bollocks.

My eyes settle on the riot of colour on my floor, the piles of red and orange and yellow. An organised rainbow of my own making and a pathetic attempt to impose order on a feeling that has none. I abandon the books, drift to the sofa, and sink into the cushions. There's a faint scent of his aftershave, a scent that clung to my sheets and my skin and now it's fading.

Rucked Up Ruse

I press my face into it like a goddamn junkie.

Finn didn't just fill the space in my flat. He filled my silences and hollows. He saw the fault lines in my defences, and, instead of exploiting them, he settled in beside me and made it feel okay to not be perfect.

I'm a caretaker and project manager. I fixed his reputation. That was the job. But he saw me, not the schedule or the polish or the woman who always has a contingency plan. He caught the slack in my smile, clocked the tremors under the surface – and *liked* it.

My fingers find the remote. I flick through channels, the noise a meaningless blur. A cooking show. A nature documentary. A game show where people are squealing with joy over a new washing machine. I let the remote fall onto the cushion beside me. Elvis hops onto my lap and nudges my chin with his head.

And that, for some reason, is the thing that finally breaks me. A deep, shuddering breath escapes me, a sound that is half sob, half gasp. I wrap my arms around my cat and nuzzle my face into his soft belly, letting the tears I'd been holding back fall. Silent, hot, and pointless.

The truth is: Finn didn't leave. I pushed him out, I told him to take the offer, because I was too scared to say what I wanted:

Please stay.

Chapter 22

Finn

My lungs are full of razors.

I'm sitting on the bench, head in my hands, trying to breathe without my chest collapsing. Every muscle screams, each joint aches. I pushed myself until the world went fuzzy at the edges, chasing an exhaustion that might finally shut my head up.

It didn't work.

I don't even remember the match. Only that we won. The changing room is a riot of steam, sweat, and twenty competing body sprays. Boots clatter on the wet tiles. Shouts echo. Connor Duff is singing something off-key about a girl from Dundee, and someone's laughing. I can't even tell who. It's a wall of sound that I can't seem to get through.

I peel the strapping from my ankle. It comes away with a rip, taking a layer of hair with it. Good, pain I can understand.

I'm still not completely sure about Marseille. But I'll probably do it. Theo and Charlie are right – it's a fantastic opportunity.

That also happens to tear my fucking heart out.

Scottie catches my eye from across the room. He frowns a

little. 'You awright, pal? Been wrestling a fucking bear, have you?'

'Just knackered.' I shove my kit into my bag with clumsy movements.

The sounds in the room swell, pressing in on me. The clank of metal, the hiss of the showers, the endless chatter.

It's too much.

Theo didn't fight for me after the meeting yesterday. She didn't even hesitate. She laid out the red carpet and pointed me towards the door. '*A fantastic opportunity,*' she said. For me. For the agency. Not for us.

Fair enough, though, because there was never an us. Not for real. Or maybe there was, but it wasn't enough to win against timing and ambition and fear.

If I were cynical, I'd say I was a project, a stray she fixed up and sent on his way with a pat on the head and a new, shinier collar. But I don't think she meant it like that. Theo's building an empire with Charlie. She deserves someone who doesn't need to be saved. Someone who's ready. I'd only get my mess all over her life.

And I'm starting to understand that loving someone doesn't mean you get to keep them, no matter how much it hurts.

'You coming to the Sin & Tonic for a burger?' Scottie asks as he pulls on a clean T-shirt.

I shake my head, gaze fixed on the floor. The tiles are a grimy black-and-white pattern. I need to get out. I want to be alone.

'Naw, got stuff to do.' I stand too fast and the room warps. I grab the edge of the locker to keep from falling.

'Finn?' Brodie sounds seriously worried.

I can't answer. I sling my bag over my shoulder and walk out, leaving the heat and the noise behind me. But the heartache follows me out.

. . .

As soon as I get home, I collapse onto my bed. My entire body still aches. Not the good ache from a tough training session, but the hurt that comes from pushing too hard to outrun your own thoughts.

I'm doom-scrolling like a twat. Instagram, TikTok, the club's official page. Pictures of me smiling in a kit I won't wear for much longer. I'm becoming a ghost in my own life. My brain fills the space with Theo's voice, the final slide of the lift doors, and the thud of my heart trying not to crumble.

I almost jump up when my phone buzzes in my hand. The screen lights up with an unknown name.

Millie.

Who the fuck is Millie?

The name rings no bells. Don't even remember saving that contact. My thumb hovers over the decline button. But the silence in the room is stronger than my desire to be left alone, so I swipe to answer and press the phone to my ear.

'Hello?' I sound appropriately gruff and suspicious.

'Finn?' The voice is plummy enough to own a pony.

'Depends on who's asking.'

A light laugh. 'It's Millie. Or Camilla. Camilla Elphinstone.'

I rack my brain. Nothing. 'Sorry, I think you've got the wrong—'

'The ski chalet? New Year's? You, me, and Olivia?' There's amusement in her voice. 'The champagne in places champagne shouldn't go?'

Ah fuck. *That* night. The one that got splashed all over the internet and media.

'I couldn't uncork the Dom Pérignon and ended up spraying it across the bedroom.'

'Right. Hi. Sorry, Camilla.' I run a hand through my damp hair. 'Took a moment.'

I like women as much as they like me, and I'm not an arsehole. But that week was one long, self-inflicted nosedive, and

I'd rather forget the whole thing. Guess I'm probably not alone with that wish. And we both know that's never gonna happen.

'Everyone calls me Millie. Except my grandmother, who insists on Camilla.'

I don't know what to say. The chalet feels like another life. Before Theo. When I was still *that* Finn – pain-drenched and drowning in distractions.

'Listen,' she continues, 'I'm ringing because there's something you have to hear. About the video.'

'What about it?'

'It was Kit. He filmed us. He's the one who sold the video to that tabloid. The highest bidder, really.'

The words hit me like a tackle I didn't see coming. Blood roar fills my ears. 'What?'

'I know, it's absurd.'

'Damn right,' I say automatically. 'Why the fuck would he do that?'

'What is it always about? Money.' Her voice is matter-of-fact. 'My family hired a private investigator to follow the money and do a full background check. Turns out dear Kit is in a spot of bother.'

I push myself up, my back hitting the headboard with a dull thud. 'What kind of bother?'

'The usual kind for boys like him,' she says, her tone breezy. 'He's in debt up to his eyeballs. Apparently, he's developed a rather expensive coke habit, and owes some unsavoury characters a great deal of money.'

Kit. With his designer clothes and trust fund. And he's broke?

I shoot to my feet and pace. 'You're sure about this?'

'Extremely. The PI found everything. Kit can't access his trust until he's twenty-seven, and Daddy cut him off. He's strapped, so he's been finding other ways to generate income to bridge the gap.'

The betrayal burns hot in my chest. Not just the filming – though that's fucked up enough – but the calculated way he'd set it up. He invited me to the chalet knowing exactly how messed up I was and used it to set the trap.

'That absolute fucking wanker,' I spit.

'Very,' Millie agrees. 'He's been doing it for years, preying on friends and acquaintances. He's well-connected, as you know. People pay to make things disappear. Or, if they can't, he sells stuff to the press.' There's a hint of hardness to her conversational tone. 'He thought we'd be easy marks.'

A cold, clean fury washes through me. 'Unbelievable.'

'I thought you'd want to know who you were dealing with.'

I drag a hand over my face. It was him. The guy who passed me the tequila, slapping me on the back.

I pace the length of my bedroom, rage building with each step. 'I'm so sorry about the video, Millie. That you got caught up in all that.'

She laughs. 'Please, don't apologise. I had a fabulous night.'

'But it's different for women,' I insist. 'The slut-shaming, the judgement. It's not okay.'

'You're right, it isn't.' The sound of her laugh bursts through, quick and bright in my ear. 'But truth be told, my family hardly blinked. The Elphinstones have centuries of well-documented scandals under their belts. A bit of a romp in a ski lodge barely registers. My great-great-grandfather once rode a horse through the lobby of the Savoy Hotel – naked – and then shat in the corner. So did the horse. Nasty opium habit. Him, not the horse.'

A smile tugs at my lips, even with the anger simmering in my gut. 'Seriously?'

'Oh yes. And that's one of the milder stories. My family was more concerned with finding the leak than our little bit of fun.' She pauses. 'How are you, though? Really?'

'I'm...' I start, then stop. What am I? Angry. Hurt. Dead inside. 'I'm surviving.'

'Your girlfriend seems lovely,' Millie says. 'I saw the photos. You look happy together.'

The mention of Theo rips open the wound I've been trying to cauterise. I don't correct Millie. Can't form the words to explain that Theo was never really mine, and it was all for show. That I fell for her anyway.

'Aye. She's... She's something else. How's Lord What's-His-Face?' I'm dying to change the subject. 'He forgive you for that night?'

'Ludo is in the past.' She sighs wearily. 'I left him and ended the engagement, actually.'

'Och, shite, hen. I'm sorry.' Am I supposed to apologise for possibly contributing to a breakup? Can't hurt, I reckon.

'Don't be. He wasn't even that upset about the sex, more about the video, which was part of the problem. He should have been with us that night instead of attending a board meeting in Luxembourg. I got a glimpse of my future and decided I'd rather not live like that.'

I sink back onto the bed. 'Good for you.'

'I should let you go. Just thought you should know about Kit. Papa's lawyers are handling it discreetly, but if you want to pursue your own legal action...'

'Thanks. I'll think about it. Say hi to your stepsister for me.'

Millie lets out a warm laugh. 'Oh, I will. She's going to be so jealous that we talked. Take care, Finn. You're a good one.'

The call ends, and I stare at my phone, emotions all over the shop. Relief that I know the truth. Rage at Kit's betrayal. A strange gratitude toward Millie for reaching out.

And beneath it all, a bone-deep hurt whenever I think of Theo.

My hands are shaking. Fucking Kit. The piece of shit who poured drinks and laughed and filmed us without consent.

Who sold me out for cash. He played us both. I can almost see his smug face. And fuck, I want to wipe that smirk off permanently.

But I'm not that man anymore.

And soon, I'll be in Marseille. Hopefully far enough away from it all. Even though it fucking wrecks me.

Chapter 23

Theo

The drive back from Elie is a long, slow exhale.

Two hours at most, I told myself. A short Sunday check-in with enough time to show face, drop off biscuits, and pretend I wasn't using the detour to hold my pieces in place.

Things with my mum have been better, in that low-grade, stable-since-seventeen way where nobody's waiting for a phone call in the night. But there's still a weight to seeing her, like stepping into a version of myself I thought I'd outgrown. Apparently, heartbreak makes me nostalgic for emotional minefields.

I could tell myself all this, and it wouldn't be wrong. But the simple truth is: I just wanted my mum.

So I stayed overnight.

The road along the coast unfolds before me like a ribbon dropped by a careless giant. The Monday morning traffic is bearable. Sunshine glints off the North Sea, turning it into a sheet of silver foil. It's not spring yet, not really, but the light's doing its best impression. One of those rare mid-February days in Scotland where the sky remembers how to be blue and everything smells faintly of potential.

I grip the steering wheel tighter. The words from an hour

ago are still ringing in my ears, bouncing around the car's quiet interior.

'I was afraid you'd harm yourself, Mum.' I said it so plainly, the sentence dropping into the space between us like a stone.

For years, that fear had been my secret roommate, the silent passenger in every car, the shadow in every room.

Mum set her teacup down with a soft click against the saucer. Her hands didn't tremble. 'Oh, sweetheart. I know, I was very unwell, but I would never have done that to you.' Her voice was calm, rooted in a balance that took her years to find.

I nodded, polite and adult, while something in me unfurled and exhaled. This is good to hear. But the younger me, the tiny, petrified project manager of our broken family, didn't know that.

The car dips and rises with the coastal road. Each curve reveals fishing villages nestled into rocky coves. Gulls are wheeling overhead, ancient church spires punctuating the sky.

'How was I supposed to know? We weren't allowed to talk about it.' I told her. 'At least I wasn't.'

The truth hung between us in her sunlit kitchen with the gingham curtains and small sculptures crowding the windowsill – rough hands cupped together, a line of heads with closed eyes, a single bird curled in on itself. She's been sculpting again for the past two years. For almost a decade, she couldn't bring herself to touch the stone.

The silence was thick with ghosts. The ghost of my dad, always away. The ghost of her depression, a stone blanket smothering every conversation. The ghost of me at thirteen, checking her breathing while she slept.

A tractor pulls out ahead, and I ease off the accelerator, welcoming the forced slowdown. The road narrows here, hedgerows pressing in on both sides, creating a green tunnel that opens suddenly to a view of fields rolling down to the sea.

Mum's depression wasn't something we ever discussed. Dad was at sea half the year, and when he was home, he pretended everything was normal. So, I became the one who made sure bills were paid, the house was clean, food was in the cupboards, and neighbours didn't get suspicious.

At thirteen, I learned to forge my mother's signature on school permission slips. By fourteen, I cooked a week's worth of meals and froze them in portions. At fifteen, I knew exactly how to answer when teachers asked why she never came to parents' evening.

Mum's face crumpled, lines appearing where there weren't any moments before. Then her arms were around me. A real hug, not the careful kind. 'I'm so sorry my illness did all that to us,' she whispered into my hair. 'To you.'

I couldn't feel my hands for a moment. Years of vigilance, of scanning rooms for signs of danger, of managing everyone's emotions before my own, all acknowledged in one sentence. And in the space of a breath, over a decade of tension began to unspool from my spine.

A flock of birds rises suddenly from a field, startled by something I can't see. They wheel and turn as one, a dark cloud against the blue sky, before settling again.

No. It wasn't fair, and it wasn't my job to carry it all alone. I was a child trying to contain a catastrophe I didn't understand. The revelation sits heavy in my chest like a boulder.

My mother got help when I was seventeen. Therapy, medication, a support group. She improved enough for me to leave for university in Edinburgh without the constant dread of what I might find when I came home. But I still spent every holiday, every free weekend at home when Dad was away with the Navy.

The road turns its back on the sea. Fields give way to small clusters of houses and, eventually, to the outskirts of

Stirling. Traffic thickens, forcing me to focus on the here and now.

By the time I pull into the car park, the sky's gone grey again, and my shoulders are locked tight. The sudden silence wraps around me.

My phone pings with a text from Charlie:

> Brodie texted me that the volunteers are about to climb your so-called boyfriend. You there?

My boyfriend, right. Yeah. The word lodges behind my breastbone, thin and precise, as if I've swallowed a pin and every breath drives it deeper. I text her back:

> Almost. 2 mins. I got this. See you later!

But do I? I check my lipstick in the rear-view mirror. Blot. Reapply. Perfect my smile until it seems good enough to fool a crowd, if not the man who's seen me lose myself beneath his hands.

The childhood that calibrated me – that made me hyper-vigilant, always scanning for emotional weather changes – also made me fantastic at my job. At reading rooms, managing crises, anticipating needs before they're voiced. But perhaps it's time to stop running everyone's emotional weather stations and live in my own climate.

I step out of the car, smoothing down my dress. In two

minutes, I have to face Finn. Three days after I let him walk away. No, since I pushed him to, and he didn't disagree.

I straighten my shoulders, lift my chin, and walk toward the venue. Time to play the part. Not the broken-hearted girlfriend he's leaving to go to France – the one who never fell in love with him to begin with.

The MacKenzie Sporting flagship store gleams with that specific retail shine, its windows filled with mannequins in overpriced activewear.

The Kick Off Kindness – Meet & Greet with the Rebels was my idea. Good for one of their biggest sponsors, good for the team, good for the agency.

There's a reason why my ex stole my ideas. They're great. And they work: the queue stretches past two storefronts on Stirling's High Street. Teenagers with phones ready, middle-aged men in jerseys, mothers with small children in oversized Rebels kit. All waiting for a glimpse of the new team in town. All waiting for the man I pushed away.

Deep breath, Theodora. Walk in like your heart isn't currently beating somewhere outside your body.

The smell hits first. New trainers and floor cleaner with overtones of nervous sweat. The acoustics amplify every sound. Shuffling feet, excited whispers.

And there he is.

Finn stands cornered by two volunteers in matching MacKenzie Sporting polos, clutching their clipboards. His hair catches the light, that pink faded to the colour of candy floss. He's nodding, lips pulled into a smile, but I recognise the tight line of his shoulders and the way his knee is bobbing.

Swallowing takes longer than it should. It's him, down to the restlessness he thinks no one notices. And somehow that's worse than seeing a stranger. It's worse because I know that body. I've kissed that jaw. And now it belongs to someone I don't get to touch anymore.

'I'm telling you, the name tag is weird smack in the middle,' one volunteer says, squinting up at his chest. 'Side placement's more natural.'

Her colleague leans in. 'Right, but… Well, everyone knows who he is. D'you reckon he even needs one?'

'Excuse me.' I step forward, professional smile clicking into place. 'Theo MacMickin, Elite Edge. Thanks for helping with the set-up.'

They turn toward me, startled and a little flustered, as if I've caught them debating whether to smack *a Hi, I'm Finn* sticker on his nipple. Which I kind of did.

'I'll take it from here,' I add smoothly, reaching for the roll of name tags on the clipboard. 'Let's go with first name, upper left. Branding stays consistent, and we keep the focus where it belongs.'

Their expressions change into careful neutrality. No one mentions why *exactly* he's so famous now that he doesn't need a name tag.

I lean in for a quick peck on the cheek, the bare minimum required for our public charade. The familiar scent of his aftershave seeps past every flimsy defence I've built since Friday. The scrape of his stubble on my neck, the sound he makes when he's close… I lock it down. He's not mine to miss.

I pull back too quickly and paste on my brightest smile. 'Let's get this show on the road, shall we?'

Chris, the store manager, appears. Anxiety radiates from every pore. 'We're ten minutes behind schedule. The queue's getting restless.'

'Everything's under control.' I scan the room. 'Where's Scottie?'

Chris' face falls. 'How should I know? Not my circus, not my monkeys.'

Rucked Up Ruse

Nothing to do about that now, so moving on. Brodie's trademark scowl is firmly in place. Jamie's beside him, lost in his phone, and his expression is as inscrutable as ever.

'Right.' I turn back to Finn. 'Ready?'

He finally meets my eyes, and I hold his gaze. It's like pressing on a bruise only to check if it still hurts. It does. It's all there. The wanting. The regret. The way he used to look at me right before he kissed me like it might kill him.

God help me. How am I supposed to survive this?

'As I'll ever be.' His voice is rougher than I remember, or maybe that's simply the way memory works, smoothing out the edges until you hear them again.

I need to say something, anything else. 'Where's Scottie?'

'He didn't come home last night.' Finn examines the trainers on the wall behind me.

'Again?'

'He's probably just shagging someone.'

'Good for him. And…also…good crowd today.' My mouth moves, but everything underneath locks up. 'Remember, extra smiles for the kids, no promises about next season, no word about the tape—'

'I know the script, Theo. I've read the memo.'

I nod briskly and turn away, clicking into work mode. Check the banners. Adjust the lighting. Brief Trish, the photographer. I won't let my personal disaster derail this event.

On my sign, the volunteers open the doors, and fans stream in, a tide of excitement washing over the store. Finn morphs into his public persona. Charming, cocky, attentive, laughing at the right moments. I watch from the periphery, acting like my heart isn't sitting on the floor somewhere between the yoga mats and kettle bells.

A young girl approaches Finn, seven or eight years old, wearing a Rebels jersey that hangs to her knees.

'You're my favourite,' she declares sternly.

Finn crouches to her level. 'That right? Well, you've got excellent taste.'

She giggles, and her eyes jump to me. 'Is that your girlfriend? I've seen the photies.'

A pulse knocks through my chest. Finn's gaze cuts to mine and skims past.

'Aye, she is,' he answers. 'Lucky me, eh?'

The girl nods solemnly. 'She's pretty.'

'The prettiest,' Finn agrees, and something in his voice pulls at a thread I'm desperately trying not to tug.

'Can I have a picture with her and you?'

Before I can formulate an excuse, Finn's looking at me again, a silent question. I nod mechanically and move beside him, careful to leave space between us.

The girl's mum positions her phone. 'Closer together, please?'

Finn places his arm around my waist, his touch is careful and precise and so professional it hurts. His palm burns through my cardigan, and I fight the urge to lean into him.

Click. A moment captured forever. His hand at my waist, my smile fixed in place, the careful distance we maintain.

'How long have you two been together?' the mother asks as she checks the photo.

The question cuts through the gap between what we are and what we almost were. How do you measure something that never really began?

'Feels like forever,' Finn answers, his tone light but his eyes serious. 'Doesn't it, *darlin'*?'

'And yet like no time at all,' I add.

The woman smiles, oblivious to the weight beneath our words. 'You make a lovely couple.'

I step away from Finn's touch, my skin still tingling where his hand rested. 'Thank you. Enjoy the rest of the event.'

The afternoon continues in this vein. Signing, photos, choreographed interactions. I move through it all on autopi-

Rucked Up Ruse

lot, a perfect simulation of efficiency. Check the time. Adjust the queue. Smile. Don't look at Finn too long. Don't fucking look at Finn at all.

Charlie arrives midway through from a meeting, surveying the scene with evident satisfaction. 'Look who it is!' she calls, weaving through the crowd. 'My brilliant partner. This is fantastic, Theo!'

I force a smile. 'We're running smoothly.'

'Absolute PR gold. Seriously. The socials are blowing up with photos of you two again.' Charlie knocks her shoulder into mine. 'We'll handle Marseille. Just think of the long-distance content we can generate until May.'

I merely nod, because if I speak, I might say the wrong thing. She moves on to Brodie.

There won't be any long-distance content.

Jamie appears at my elbow, his usual stoic expression softened by something like concern. 'You awright?'

'Fine,' I reply automatically. 'Why?'

He shrugs. 'Finn's been awfy quiet, and that's not like him.'

'Maybe he's tired.'

Jamie studies me a moment too long. 'Maybe.'

Trish, the photographer, catches my attention, gesturing toward Finn. 'Can we get a cute couple shot? Only the two of you?'

Again? Dread zips down my spine. 'Is that necessary?'

'Kind of. It's for the new press kit.' She smiles.

Of course. I wrote that brief myself, weeks ago. Back when pretending to be Finn's girlfriend wasn't slowly suffocating me.

Yep. I'm the creator of my own undoing.

I approach Finn, who's finished signing a rugby shirt with his number eight. 'They want a photo with us.'

He nods, gaze locked down like a vault. 'Where do you want me?'

In my arms. In my bed. In my fucking life.

'By the banner,' I say, pointing to the *Kick Off Kindness* display. 'Good branding opportunity.'

We position ourselves side by side, but Trish frowns. 'Could you stand closer, your arm around her?'

Finn's hand hovers low on my back. There, but not touching. It sets me on fire, and I want to scream.

'One more,' Trish says. 'Look at each other this time?'

I turn toward Finn as he turns to me. Our eyes lock, and for a second, the store, the crowd, the whole charade falls away. There's only him and his sky-blue eyes that see too much.

'Theo,' he says, so quietly only I can hear.

'Don't,' I whisper back. Because if he says anything real, anything true, I'll fall to pieces right here under the fluorescent lights.

The flash goes off, we both blink, and the spell breaks.

'Perfect.' Trish reviews the shot with a grin. 'That's the one.'

I step away, pulling my phone from my pocket. 'I need to check some emails. Excuse me.'

I don't wait for his response, just turn and stride toward the back office, each step measured and controlled. Calm, composed, and absolutely not shattering inside.

The back room is full of boxes of merchandise and a desk cluttered with invoices. I sink into the chair, hands shaking as I set down my phone. Today isn't just hard because I'm pretending to be with someone I pushed away.

It's hard because I'm pretending not to love someone I do.

I stood next to him not two minutes ago, and every cell in my body exhaled like it had been waiting. Being close to him – feeling the heat of his body, hearing his breath hitch when I leaned in – cracked something wide open. He looked at me like it still hurt. And it did. For both of us. But being that close again... God, it felt like the first right thing in ages.

Rucked Up Ruse

Finn is the only thing that makes sense.

I'm in love with him.

Sweet Jesus, I'm in love with Finn Lennox.

And I urged him to leave for France without even asking him if that's what he wants. I pushed him away and closed the door on him, like his mother did.

Shit, I cocked this up so hard. There's no coming back from that. For the first time in my life, I don't know what to do. I don't know how to fix this.

I'm not a fixer, I'm a mess and it's all my fault.

That's when the tears come.

That's also when the door creaks. I wipe my cheeks with both hands and sit taller. The footsteps stop directly behind my chair.

'There you are! Thought I saw you disappear.' Charlie's voice has this deep tinge of someone who's clearly successful and thoroughly satisfied. Twice daily, based on her glow.

I blink rapidly at my phone screen, pretending to be working on a social posting.

'Are you okay, Theo?'

I nod without turning around, desperately willing my face to reset itself. 'Oh, aye. Just fine-tuning the wording for—'

'Theodora.' Her tone softens with concern.

'Charlotte.' I spin slowly, and her grin dies.

'Fuck.' She kicks the door shut behind her. 'What happened?'

'Allergies.' My voice breaks. 'And a new moisturiser.'

Charlie crouches, peering up at me. Gold hoops glint. 'Try again.'

'Period cramps?'

'Bollocks. We're kind of synced since we've started working together, and I'm not due for another two weeks.' She grips my shoulders. 'Theo.'

The harsh light spits its artificial glow into every corner of the cluttered storeroom.

A stifled hiccup escapes. 'It's nothing.'

Before I can fabricate another lie, she's crouched in front of me, arms wrapping around my shoulders. The dam breaks again, and I'm sobbing into pristine, champagne-coloured silk.

'I'm ruining your blouse,' I mumble against her torso between sobs.

'I don't give a shit.' She pulls back. 'Talk to me. Now.'

I take a shuddering breath. 'It wasn't supposed to be real.'

'What wasn't?' She hands me a tissue from her purse, one of those fancy ones that smell of lavender.

'The relationship. Finn. Us. It was meant to be a rebrand strategy and a business arrangement.'

'Oh.' She sits on a nearby box of trainers, her expression unfolding from confusion to understanding. 'And it became something else.'

'*Everything* else.' The words tumble out, raw and unfiltered. 'He's not who I thought he was, Charlie. Not even close.'

'So who is he then?'

I fiddle with the crumpled tissue. 'He's funny and kind and attentive. Completely lacking in self-preservation. He notices things. How I take my tea, when I'm overthinking. He's a complete disaster at loading a dishwasher, but he'll spend ten minutes making sure Elvis has the perfect blanket nest.'

'Wait, what?' Charlie lifts her eyebrows. 'Your cat gremlin hates everyone.'

'I know! But not him. And he's so...' I draw a useless circle in the air, trying to sum him up, 'genuine. Even when he's being an absolute fanny, he's honest about it.'

'Unlike some people I know.' She pins me with a look that's half affection, half indictment.

'What's that supposed to mean?'

Rucked Up Ruse

'It means you're the queen of compartmentalisation, Theo. You've got thicker walls than Edinburgh Castle.'

I wince. 'That's not—'

'Fair? Maybe not. True? Dead on. Takes one to know one.' She squeezes my knee. 'So what happened?'

'Marseille happened. This partnership happened.' I wipe fresh tears from my cheeks. 'And I told him to go because it was the right move for his career. And for the agency.'

'Hmm.' Charlie's hum contains multitudes of judgement.

'Don't "hmm" me like that. I was being professional.'

'Nonsense. You were being scared.'

'I thought he'd never stay anyway; that's not his thing.'

'How do you know it couldn't become his thing? No, you told him to go because you thought you weren't allowed to ask for what you want. And if you did, and he said he'd go anyway, your squishy heart wouldn't survive it.'

The damp tissue disintegrates between my fingertips. 'Sounds not entirely implausible.'

Charlie leans closer, her voice dropping. 'And now it all makes sense.'

'What does?'

'For starters, that Finn told me two minutes ago he won't sign Marseille.'

My heart stops. 'He said what now?'

'Yeah, he said he doesn't feel ready to leave the Rebels. It's a new team, and he wants to finish what he started. At least this season, but preferably until they're at the top. Said he's not a quitter.' Her eyes twinkle. 'But I'm beginning to see that he's not only staying for the Rebels, but for my brilliant, beautiful, kind-hearted partner.'

I gape at her. 'You're making that up.'

'I'm not.' Charlie raises her right hand. 'Brownie's honour.'

'You were never a brownie.'

'Details.' She waves dismissively. 'The point is, he's staying in Stirling.'

I blink. That wasn't the plan.

'I'm going to ask you what you asked me last year.' She moves, and the cardboard box creaks beneath her. 'Did he do anything to hurt you, ignore you, treat you like shit? What did he actually do wrong?'

'Not a single thing.' I keep staring at the scuffed linoleum.

'Partner,' she says with a grin that's half triumph, half sympathy, 'you're in love with him.'

'I know, dammit.' I swipe at my face with the back of my hand. 'But what I don't know is when you got so good at that?'

Charlie kisses my cheek. 'I learned from the best. You told me that love can be a superpower. Remember?'

I nod, recalling how I gave her that pep talk when the thing with Brodie went down.

'The thing is, you can't control love, Theo. And that's scary. But,' she adds with a smirk, 'when you lose control with someone safe, it sets you free. Ask me how I know.'

'I'd really rather not.' But I feel my lips curl upward despite everything.

Charlie pulls another tissue out and hands it to me. 'Do you know why I made you my partner?'

I dab at my eyes and blow my nose like an elephant in the Edinburgh zoo. 'Because I'm the best and always have a plan?'

'No.' She shakes her head. 'Because you're at your best when you don't have a plan. When the script goes out the window and you improvise... That's when you shine. Might be time to bin the spreadsheets and go off-script.'

I know she's right. And I know I'm in love with him. But I've already shoved him away once, and I won't go charging back in without a way to undo the damage.

Chapter 24

Finn

Turns out, heartbreak tastes exactly the same as a cold pizza at midnight.

The light in our flat share has gone the colour of dishwater. I've been sitting in the same spot on the sofa for two hours, watching the shadows creep across the walls. It's too quiet. Scottie's out somewhere again, leaving me with an army of demons and hellscapes of intrusive thoughts.

I've got the telly on – some quiz show with too much shouting and zero brain cells – but I'm not watching it. The volume's high enough to cover the silence, but it still feels like I'm echoing.

I grab a slice of pizza from the box on the coffee table and lean back. It's dry, and the cheese has set like rubber. I eat it anyway.

Four days since she was right next to me at the MacKenzie event. Four days of replaying every second, every micro-expression that crossed her face.

She looked good.

Although... She looked breakable underneath that shell. Untouchable. Every inch of her a line I used to be allowed to cross. That soft perfume she wears, the one that makes my IQ drop with every inhale. She tried not to look at me directly. But when our eyes met, I saw a flash of hurt before the walls slammed back up.

But she didn't waver when we took that picture. Held herself steady beside me, shoulder to shoulder as though we hadn't been naked in her bed a week ago, making promises with our bodies we weren't brave enough to speak out loud.

I'd told myself I could handle this event. A bit of PR. Flash a smile. Sign a jersey. Pretend I'm not splitting at the seams inside.

Lie of the fucking year.

Today is Valentine's Day, and she's posted a photo of us on my socials. Her all glowing and gorgeous, me looking at her like she hung the bloody moon. And it makes me want to punch a wall, kiss her senseless, and throw up in the same breath.

I get up with a groan and drag myself to the kitchen, flicking on lights as I go. The refrigerator offers slim pickings: half a block of cheddar with suspicious blue spots and milk that's a day from walking out on its own. There's a beer in the back. I don't take it.

Behind a half-empty takeaway container, I find a lone can of Irn Bru. I open it with one hand, and the sweet taste hits my tongue. When I shut the fridge, my dull reflection winks back in the steel.

Silly bastard.

Marseille would've been easier, I think as I make my way back to the couch. Sunshine, clean slate, fresh start, life-changing money, and security. Everything I never had growing up. Theo wanted me to take it.

And I nearly did.

But then I saw her at the signing. Putting on an act for the cameras, answering questions she hated, pretending we were still something. She's got this way of carrying other people's weight without ever letting them see her knees buckle.

Rucked Up Ruse

I just stood there, being looked at like I was hers.

And I'm not.

But I know that If I'd gone to Marseille, I'd be rich and miserable. I'd be a quitter with a tan. I'm tired of packing up my damage and calling it reinvention, of leaving when things get hard.

I take my phone out of my pocket and unlock it. Charlie's text from yesterday still sits there:

> You better be serious about staying. I staked my name on you. Don't make me regret it.

I won't.

I said say no to Marseille because I couldn't stomach the thought of being in another country while Theo MacMickin walked through life, shouldering it all, pretending she can do it all and we never mattered.

I know she doesn't ask for anything, and she won't ever say she needs me.

But I'll be here for her anyway.

I'm staying for Theo, even if she doesn't want me to. Even if the next few months of our 'relationship' are pure theatre. Performance. I'm desperate enough to take what I can get.

Pathetic doesn't even begin to cover it.

It's fucking ironic: from faking I loved her to faking I don't.

I scrub a hand over my face. Skin sandpapered, brain splintered. I need to shave. Need to sleep.

The thing is, I simply can't get on a plane to France knowing I'd be running away. From the team that gave me a chance. From Theo, who believed in me when I was nothing but a PR disaster with a porn tape. So yeah, I'm also staying because I need to prove something. To Charlie, to the team, to myself. That I can stick with something even when it gets tough.

And it's tough now, Christ, it's brutal. Training with a heart that's torn down the middle, smiling for the press when all I want to do is crawl into bed and stay there.

But I'm going to make it work. I'll pull my shit together. I'll bag another brand, a proper one. If I bring in a deal, I prove I'm not dead weight. Not to the team, not to the agency. And not to the woman who saw something in me before I knew it was there. Even if she doesn't want me, I'll be around. I'll be here for her.

I toss the pizza crust in the box.

I'll show her I've got loyalty in me too. Theo's loyalty is relentless. She bleeds for people, cleans up after them, and makes sure the carpet doesn't stain. I want to be the kind of man who deserves that.

Who deserves her.

And I can't be that man in Marseille.

The telly howls into the silence. I stab the remote, and the flat collapses into quiet. I scroll on my phone and let the algorithm spoon-feed me other people's nights out and filtered lives.

Scroll. Swipe. Double tap.

And then I see him.

Kit Lascelles-Finch.

I should've blocked that motherfucker. But I didn't. And now Kit's face fills my screen. He's leaning on wrought-iron railings – cigarette in hand, velvet jacket slung over his shoulder – outside a tall, nondescript Georgian townhouse with pillars. A single plaque on the wall reads *Members Only* in matte brass.

The tagged location: The Wolf Room. Edinburgh New Town.

So that's where he's slithering right now. I've heard the

name before, a place where the rich go to misbehave and never get caught.

I watch the story one more time.

My pulse is in my teeth. The room's too small to hold the heat boiling under my skin. There's nothing I can fix with Theo. No undoing it, no rewinding the last few days. But I can do this.

So I grab my keys.

There's the brass plaque, a velvet rope, and a wall of silence behind it. Two doormen in matching suits guard the entrance like it's MI5. Not bulky lads either. Lean, quiet, and dead serious. You don't get bounced from this place, you get erased.

I clock the scanner wand tucked behind the door frame. No one's walking in here with a phone or an ounce of shame.

I nod once. 'Evenin'.'

The one on the left gives me a once-over, not impressed. The one on the right narrows his eyes as if he's trying to place me but can't decide if I belong in the papers or on the list or both.

'You on the book?' Left one asks.

'Not officially,' I say.

Then the bouncer on the right recognises me. His mouth stays still, but I see the little click behind his eyes when the penny drops. 'Finn Lennox?'

'Aye, the very one.'

'My wee brother's a fan. Strong season.'

'Thanks, man.'

He nods, reaching for the drawer behind him. I don't have to flash anything, my face does the job.

'Phone,' he says, and I hand it over. He locks it in one of those rubber sleeves with a snap, drops it into the drawer, and unhooks the rope. 'No photos. No names. No trouble.'

'No promises.' I say with a wink. Can't help myself.

The rope falls, the door swings wide, and I walk into the dark.

Inside, the air presses in. Everything is low-lit and deliberate, curated to feel secretive. Music pulses from the walls.

I don't hang about.

I cut through a corridor lined with smoked mirrors and no reflections I want to see and step into something that looks like a red-lit fever dream. Booths sunken into walls, half-pulled curtains hiding sins no one's pretending to regret. Champagne is sweating in silver buckets, glittering watches are flashing as hands wander. Laughter pitched just low enough to make you wonder what it's covering. It's a depraved playground where bad behaviour's the whole fucking point, so they don't bother pretending to be good.

There's Kit, lounging like a Roman emperor mid-orgy. Centre of his own little solar system. Shirt half undone, mouth curled as if he's said something clever. High as a fucking kite. He's got a hand on a girl's knee and another wrapped around a whisky tumbler.

Probably paid for with that fucking sex tape he made of me, Millie, and Olivia.

My vision tunnels, and pressure needles the backs of my eyeballs. The bass drops out, and all I feel is the grind of my teeth and the throbbing urge to drive him through the wall.

He sees me, eventually. The second I step into his line of sight, the grin twitches.

'Well, well. Scotland's favourite redemption story,' he drawls, like we're old pals grabbing pints after training. 'Didn't think you'd be allowed in here, old chap. Dress code and all that.'

'We need to talk.'

He pushes up from the booth in that spoilt way of his, slow and fluid, as if he's never had to rush for anything in his life.

Rucked Up Ruse

I stop in front of him, close enough to smell the whisky on his breath. 'I want to hear it from you. Did you leak it?'

His gaze is drifting somewhere over my shoulder. I'm boring him already. 'Leak what, Lennox?'

'Don't piss about. The video. You set us up.'

He sips from his crystal tumbler as if we're at a garden party. 'Christ, at least buy me a drink first. Or is this another one of your public meltdowns?'

That's his trick, reframe fury as hysteria, so any counter-punch makes you the unstable one. I know the script.

When I speak, my voice is quieter than the ice clinking in his glass. Cold, too. 'You filmed us without consent. Sold it. Let us carry the fallout while you sat here polishing your fucking cufflinks.'

He rolls his eyes. 'What exactly do you think this is, Finn? A morality tribunal? You got caught shagging in a chalet with a nanny cam hidden in a teddy bear. Boo fucking hoo. Half the lads in this place have done worse this week. Don't make a fuss. You're a fuck up by nature, already sliding downhill. I merely gave you a nudge.'

A hot wire of rage scorches up my throat, logic burned away. 'Sliding, was I? Funny that I'm still standing. Unlike you, I sorted my shit, and now I know exactly who pushed me. No one drags me or the people I care about through the gutter, you rancid wee fuck.'

'Oh, I see. You're doing the whole reformed act. Righteous boyfriend now, is it? Playing knight for your little missus?'

My blood's howling for revenge. His face, my fist, the wall. Doesn't matter. Just break something. He doesn't know Theo, he's never met her. But of course, he's seen the photos, and he's seeing the look on my face, so he decided to aim straight for it.

Sick bastard.

Kit smiles, ripe with rotted charm. 'They always go for the broken ones, don't they? The ones with a saviour complex?

Sweet of her, really. Being the girlfriend of a rabid dog on a lead.'

He's off his face, can't even keep his pupils still. I start to turn away with gritted teeth. That piece of shite isn't worth it.

He sniffs and rolls his shoulder. 'Hope she knows what she's doing. Wouldn't want her ending up just another dumb bitch in your next video.' He laughs. 'Phone me when you're done. Would love a turn before you chuck her.'

My whole body goes still. Heat floods my ears. The room tilts.

'What the fuck did you just say?'

Chapter 25

Theo

The call comes at 2:07 am. No good news comes at this time – especially not from an unknown caller. I fumble upright, knock over a glass of water, and answer on the third ring, heart already banging against my ribs.

'Theo MacMickin.'

There's a pause on the other end. It makes my stomach brace before my brain catches up.

Then: 'It's me.'

I sit bolt upright. 'Finn?'

He sighs, the sound is low and defeated. 'Didn't mean to wake you. I called the agency. Got forwarded to your number, I guess.'

He's guessing correctly. Charlie's off-grid for her monthly date weekend with Brodie, which means I'm emergency coverage. That's usually a missed flight or a schedule mix-up in a different time zone, if anything.

Clearly not as simple as that when Finn Lennox is involved.

I let out a groan. 'What's going on?'

'You won't like it. I'm…not exactly tucked up in bed.'

'Where the hell are you?' I'm already swinging my legs out of bed.

'Police station in Edinburgh. St Leonard's.'

'What the fuck?' My feet hit the floor. 'Jesus. Are you okay?'

'Mostly. You should see the other guy.' He tries for a laugh, but it comes out more like a cough.

I sit there, phone wedged between my shoulder and ear. Blood drains to my feet. 'That's not funny! Are you injured?'

'Not really. Just a small… It was…' He clears his throat. 'Breach of the peace. Got into it with a guy in a club. Nothing serious. They're keeping us for a wee while, cooling-off thing. No charges.'

There's a rustle of movement on his end. Footsteps. A murmur of some other voice I can't make out.

I reach for the hoodie on the chair. 'What does "got into it" mean? And what sort of club?'

'The Wolf Room.'

I stop moving. That's not a club, it's a cesspit for fucked-up behaviour. Rich-kid depravity. 'Dammit, Finn!'

I press the heel of my hand to my forehead. I should be asleep, dreaming of inbox zero. Instead, I'm getting dressed in the wee hours to pick a rugby player up from St Leonard's. And not any old rugby player – the one who wormed his way into my heart and knickers and life.

'Are you mad?'

'Och, Lennox!' I unzip my make-up bag. Stare into it. Close it again. 'Is there press?'

'Not that I can tell. Quiet night so far.'

My brain starts rearranging itself as I hop into the hallway on one leg, pulling my joggers up. Priorities, logistics, optics. But under that…terror. The helpless fury that only comes when someone you care about gets into trouble and you weren't there to stop it.

Rucked Up Ruse

And beneath that a shocking clarity. I'd do anything for him, no questions asked.

Until now, I had no clue what it meant being ready to bury a body for someone. There are few people I'd pick up from a police station in the middle of the night.

And Finn Lennox is right at the top of that list.

I don't know what I'm going to say to him when I get there. If I slap or shake or kiss him. But he's alone and angry, hurt, probably a bit scared.

So I'm on my way.

My keys are already in my hand. 'I'll be there in twenty. Do not speak to anyone else.'

'Theo, I didn't know this call would... You really don't have to—'

'Shut up. Your call landed here. That means I'm the one who shows up, and that's that.'

He exhales. 'Okay. Thank you.'

I hang up, grab my bag, rush into the kitchen, reach above the microwave where I keep the emergency shortbread tin, and shove it in the bag.

A girl can't pick up her man from the cells without biscuits.

The waiting room of St Leonard's police station reeks of bleach. My keys dig into my palm as I perch on a plastic chair. My brain is a pinball machine of worst-case scenarios. He's been arrested. His career is over. Our deal is over. He's hurt. He's...

A harsh buzz slices through the quiet, followed by the heavy clank of a magnetic lock releasing. A door at the end of the corridor swings open.

Finn comes in like he's braced for impact.

There's a sudden vacuum where my breath should be. He

looks fucking miserable. A raised, angry-red bump swells beneath a fresh scrape. His eyes are bloodshot, and the first hints of a bruise are starting to bloom above his brow. He moves with a weariness that has nothing to do with the hour, holding a sealed pouch in his right hand. I assume that's his personal belongings.

Every ounce of my composure evaporates. My feet move, and I don't stop until I collide with his chest, my arms wrapping around his torso, pulling him into a hug that's more about not falling apart than an embrace. He's warm and solid and stiffens for a second, then melts into me, his arms coming around my back to hold me just as tightly.

That's all I needed. That right here.

I almost cry.

'You stupid bampot,' I mumble into his shirt. 'What have you done?'

He rests his chin on the crown of my head, a deep sigh shuddering through his frame. 'It's okay, darlin'. I'll tell you outside. But you're not gonna like it.'

I pull back, my hands still gripping his arms, and search his face. As I take in the damage, a fresh wave of fury and fear washes over me. 'Has anyone ever been elated to pick someone up from a holding cell?'

Then I grab his big, strong hand, and wrap my fingers through his without thinking.

I give a sharp tug and pull him toward the exit. 'Come. You can explain yourself in the car, Mister.'

For three minutes, the only sounds are the rhythmic swish of the windscreen wipers and the clicks of the indicator as I navigate the sleeping city. Edinburgh's streetlights smear across the wet tarmac in long, orange streaks.

I will not speak first. I will not.

Every red light bathes us in crimson, turning his bruised

face into something from a horror film. He lets out another gusty, world-weary sigh that could deflate a bouncy castle and rattles the last of my patience.

'Will you stop moaning and explain what happened?' The words burst out of me. 'Or shall I drive around in circles until morning?'

He rubs one large hand along his jaw, a nervous habit I've catalogued alongside his twenty others. 'It's complicated.'

'Ah, complicated. You've been detained by police at a members-only sex club, and *complicated* is the best you can offer?'

'It's not a sex club.' He pauses. 'I don't think.'

I take a corner too sharply, the car lurching. 'Oh, well that's better then.'

He drops his head back. 'I found out who leaked the tape.'

My foot slips on the accelerator. 'What?'

'Kit Lascelles-Finch.' His voice hardens around the name. 'One of the – individuals, as you phrased it in your press release – in the video contacted me. Said Kit recorded us and sold it for cash.'

'And you thought confronting him there was a wise solution?' I navigate around a delivery van. 'What about letting a solicitor handle it?'

He has the grace to look ashamed. 'I wasn't planning anything. Just saw in his Instagram story where he was, and I snapped.'

My brain clicks back into strategy mode. 'He confessed? We have a witness? That's fantastic. We can sue him into the next century. Defamation, breach of privacy... Oh, that's going to be some juicy legal action.' I try to sound professional when all I really want to do is find Kit and run him over with my Fiat. 'Revenge porn is illegal in Scotland. Recording without consent—'

'Naw.' Finn cuts me off and shakes his head, his gaze fixed

on the road ahead. 'The guy's a mess, Theo. A sad, sleazy bastard. He's fucked enough as is.'

'You're *defending* him?'

'I'm not defending him. I'm just saying I don't want to spend the next year of my life in court with him.'

I turn onto Queen's Drive, the road curving upward. Finn frowns, peering out the window. 'Wait. Where are we driving? That's not where my car is, and that's definitely not the way to Leith.'

'I think it's high time that we talk.' The words come out way steadier than I feel. 'And I know the best spot.'

He doesn't argue, just watches the city lights spread out below us as the car climbs.

'So, Lennox – what *exactly* occurred in that sinkhole for the financially advantaged and morally compromised?'

'Found him in a booth and told him I knew what he'd done and what a disgusting, blackmailing cunt he is.' A pause. 'Was planning to leave it at that.'

'But…?'

'But he said something as I was walking away.' His voice drops. 'And I lost it.'

We're approaching Blackford Hill now, the dome of the Royal Observatory visible against the night sky. I pull into the small car park, and kill the engine. The sudden silence feels heavy. Below us, Edinburgh is a constellation of gold and white lights against the deep black of the Firth of Forth.

'What do you mean, "something" and "lost it"? Elaborate.'

Finn stares straight ahead, his profile sharp in the dim light. His jaw works, as if he's chewing on words he doesn't want to say.

I reach into the back seat, grab the tin of shortbread, and shove it into his hands. 'Here. Eat and tell me everything.'

He pries open the lid, takes a biscuit, and puts it back without taking a bite. His eyes meet mine. 'He insulted you. And I head-butted him.'

Rucked Up Ruse

I glare at him, unable to process the words. 'You...*head-butted* him?' I repeat slowly. 'Because he *insulted* me?'

Finn nods, the movement small and tight.

'You got yourself arrested,' my voice rises with each syllable, 'risked your career and everything we've worked for because a bully said something mean about me?'

'Aye. I don't care what it costs me. Nobody talks about you like that.'

'How old are you? Six?' I stare at him, mouth slightly open, brain buffering.

He shrugs, his eyes on the skyline as if this isn't the most confusing night of either of our lives. 'He deserved it.'

'Oh, no doubt. Grade A arsehole. But this is not medieval Scotland, and you do not have to defend my honour with brute force. You're lucky that this kind of club doesn't allow cameras or mobiles.'

His head turns. Slowly. 'Wasn't really a pro-and-con decision, Theo. He riled me up.'

'Riled you up?' My voice squeaks on the word you. 'You're a professional athlete.'

'I won't let anyone speak about you like that. Not in my presence. Ever.'

The words drop like bricks. No apology. Just that flat, gritty conviction in his voice. It should piss me off. It really should. But something strange happens inside me instead. I go weirdly floaty and warm. As if I've swallowed a hot-water bottle.

My fingers twitch on my knee. 'Why?'

The hard edge of his expression drops, and the cocky, stubborn mask falls away. What remains is raw, unguarded pain. 'Because I fucking love you, and I don't know how to stop!'

Something in my chest fractures. Sternum? Heart? I don't know. I just know I can't stop shaking.

'I had no idea love would do that to me, because I clearly

have never been in love, but it does. I love you, and I will strangle anyone with my bare fucking hands if they ever say something mean about you or hurt you.'

'What did you just say?' I whisper.

He blinks. 'That I'll strangle—'

'No. Before that.'

'I love you, Theo.'

There it is again. Out in the open. No jokes or caveats. My heart lurches, and my vision fuzzes at the edges. Edinburgh's lights blur beneath us. The car suddenly feels too small, too hot, too everything.

'I love how your brain works three steps ahead of everyone else's. I love how you fix everything without taking credit. I love your lists. And your tits. Not necessarily in that order.'

My lungs have forgotten their one job.

'I love how you make everyone feel safe,' he continues, each word gaining momentum. 'That you bring shortbread to police stations at two-thirty in the morning.' He gestures at the tin. 'I mean, who does that?'

'I do,' I whisper.

'Aye. You. I've never met anyone like you. And I tried so hard not to love you, I swear. But you're...' He runs a hand through his hair, searching for words. 'You're a part of my soul. And I have no idea how you got there.'

I try to laugh, but it comes out wet. My eyes sting.

'I didn't go to Marseille because of you,' he continues. 'I couldn't.'

'But the money, your career—'

'Fuck the money. I'd rather be here, fighting for something real, than rich, alone, and miserable in France.'

Another tear escapes, and this time I don't bother wiping it away. 'You can't make career decisions based on…on…'

'Love? Watch me.' The corner of his mouth lifts. 'Say something, Theo.'

Rucked Up Ruse

'So you're really staying? For good?'

'Aye. Was always going to, baby.'

'Finn...' I take a shaky breath. 'I think I love you, too?'

'Is that a question? I thought you don't do uncertainty.'

'I've never felt something like this before, so I don't have enough data.' My voice wobbles. 'The sample size is limited.'

'Shut up, List Girl.' He reaches across the centre console, his hands gentle as they frame my face. 'You're the smartest, kindest, most loyal, fucking sexy woman I've ever met.' He leans in. 'And I'm done pretending I'm not gone for you.'

His mouth is on mine before I can even respond. And it's not a soft kiss. It's bruising and filthy with need, messy and aching and real. The handbrake jabs my leg, but I'm long past caring about anything other than him.

I make a tiny sound in my throat. My body knows *exactly* what it wants.

'I didn't mean to fall for you, Finn. But here I am.'

'Well, tough shite, MacMickin. Because I'm all in. You hear me? All in.'

Both of us are still breathless. My lips are tingling from the kiss. If you can call it a kiss; it felt more like a claim and detonation. I sit there, straddling the line between dizzy and starving, my thighs clenched tight, my brain glitching in multiple directions. He's here. And he loves me.

Finn Lennox loves me.

I need him. Now. Right here.

He draws back an inch. His eyes search mine. 'You okay, darlin'?'

I nod. Then shake my head. 'No. Yes. Fuck.' My hands fist in the front of his hoodie. 'Do you even know what you do to me?'

'Theo...'

'I'm serious. You walk into a room, and my brain abandons all logic. I can't help myself.'

His lips part on a chuckle, but I'm not done.

'And sure, it might set feminism back a century, but the fact that you'd go to jail for me? That does things to me I'm not proud of.'

I'm already moving before I know I've made the decision. Unbuckling my seatbelt, shifting up to climb over the centre console. It's graceless and greedy. I nearly elbow him in the throat.

He catches me by the hips. 'Jesus, Theo. What are you—'

'I love how you smell. I love your pink hair and your tattoos and your unicorn sleeping mask. I love how you look at me and that you drink my matcha.'

My knees sink either side of his thighs. I'm in his lap now, and I can feel exactly how this is affecting him.

'I've never needed anyone the way I need you.' I kiss the tip of his nose, his left cheek. 'It's infuriating. But it's true.'

He exhales through his nose. 'Say that again.'

'I need you, Finn. So much that I'm dying without you.' And then I take his face into my hands and kiss him again.

He groans, a low sound from deep in his chest, and suddenly we're nothing but limbs and mouths and scraped-up emotion.

'You want to fuck right here, baby? In this tiny car in a car park in February?'

'What's the saying again? Love finds a way?' I mumble as I'm reaching into his joggers, pulling him free.

He hisses through his teeth as I wrap my fingers around his rigid length. 'Dammit, Theo…'

The warmth of him fills my palm and touching him again feels like I've swallowed an electric shock. 'I want you,' I say, my nose brushing his. 'All of you. Nothing between us.'

Finn's breath skates harsh against my mouth. I'm trembling, actually trembling, and it's not the cold. My skin's burning, tight with need and desperation.

He freezes. One hand still fisted in my joggers, the other

splayed low on my back. 'Theo... Christ, darlin', wait. You clean?'

'Y-yes. You?'

'Aye. Always tested, always bagged up.' His voice is hoarse as he drags his lips down my neck, teeth grazing that spot that makes me sigh. 'You on something?'

I nod, dragging my mouth across his cheek, tasting salt and heat and skin. 'Pill.'

He growls. *Growls*. His head tips back, hits the seat with a dull thud. 'You're letting me in raw, Theo?'

'Yes. Now. Or I'm going to scream so loud I'll wake the whole of Edinburgh.'

That pulls a laugh from him. Broken and unbelieving. 'Wee menace.'

He kisses me again, his teeth knock mine, our mouths sliding wet and open and frantic. Then he dives his hand between us, past the waistband of my joggers. Calluses catch, then glide. Two fingers pushing in with the same pressure as a blade sinking into softened butter, and he groans when I clench around him. The rough texture of his skin, the exact right friction has me choking out a moan. He curses softly, fingertips stroking gently once, twice, spreading me open, and every nerve in my body sings in response.

'Fuck, Theo. This is how much you love me?'

'Yes. Yes!'

There's no plan. Just this flailing urgency to *prove* it. To fuse what we just said with skin. With sweat and kisses and sex and love.

I scramble back on shaking knees, as I drag one leg free of my joggers. My knickers stick to my skin, stretched to the side, useless. The windows are fogged.

He spits in his hand and rubs it on his cock, thick and waiting. He holds it, eyes locked to mine. 'You want it slow, baby?'

'If you go slow, I'll bite you.'

He lets out a low laugh. One hand holds my hip, the other fists his cock. 'Take me, then.'

I lower myself and gasp so hard my throat hurts.

Oh.

Oh my fucking god.

He's big. Stretching me open, dragging against every nerve as I sink down. I cry out, forehead crashing to his shoulder as my body adjusts, burning and needy and alive.

He swears into my hair, both hands gripping my hips so hard I'll wear the bruises for days. We're not moving yet. Just breathing and trembling.

'Jesus, Theo.' His voice is a rasp. 'You feel like… fuck. I've never—'

'Shush.' I shiver as I bottom out, hips flush to his. 'Or I'll start crying again.'

He fills every inch of me, pressure and pleasure and a feeling too big for my chest to contain.

'Good,' he buries his face in my neck. 'Want you ruined for everyone else.'

I want to ruin *him*, too. Want him to carry this inside him like a fever. Like proof that I chose him back. That I'm not walking away.

I move. Tiny moves at first, rolling my hips. 'You feel that?' I whisper against his throat. 'That's how much I want you. That's how much I *missed* you.'

His hands grip my arse, guiding me. 'I missed you, too, baby. So much.'

Mouths open, gasping, pressed together. We can't get close enough.

'I love you. Theo… I love you so much it fucking *hurts*.'

'I love you. I love you, Finn.'

Every time I move, there's the sticky drag of him inside me, the whimper I can't contain, the ragged groans he tries to muffle in my neck.

Rucked Up Ruse

'You feel so good, baby,' he mutters into my skin.

'Don't stop talking.'

'Why? This turning you on?'

'Everything about you turns me on.' I grind down again, harder this time. 'The way you look at me. The way you... *fuck*, Finn!'

He thrusts up suddenly, meeting me halfway. 'That it?' His eyes are blown wide, locked on my face. 'That what you need?'

'Yes! More. Just...don't stop...'

He's pounding up into me now, hard and deep, and it's everything I've ever wanted. The car rattles.

'I love you,' I gasp. 'I think I've always... *fuck*... Ah!'

The sounds – panting, the rhythm of skin meeting skin – fill the car. I'm so close. And he knows it.

'Good girl. Prove how much you missed me. Come on my cock.'

He drops a hand to my clit and rubs, tight circles, and I sob out a sound I don't recognise. My body locks up and *shatters*, everything contracting around him. He doesn't stop, grabs my hips, and fucks up into me like he's chasing his last breath. I cry out, loud and raw, no filter, no shame.

'Yes, Theo... Fuck, I love you!'

I feel him swell, pulse, throbbing inside me as he comes, filling me with heat so intense I moan again. His arms crushing me to him as if the world might split apart.

He holds me, and we stay there. One.

For a long moment, we just breathe, wrapped in heat and sweat and love. The world beyond the car doesn't exist. It's just us and the words we can't take back. I'm still panting, my body wrecked, my heart wide open. This is the most reckless, feral thing I've ever done. And somehow, the most honest.

The most me.

Who'd have thought that *Operation Dummy Pass* would lead to the biggest try of my life?

'Wow.' I drop my head to his shoulder, heart thundering and overflowing. 'Happy Valentine's day, by the way... Are you okay?'

'I'll never be okay again without you.' Finn cradles my face. 'So no. I'm not okay, Theo. I'm yours.'

Epilogue

Finn

Four and a half months later...

The whistle blows and the season dies.

We lost. The final score flashes up on the big screen. A bright, digital insult. Glasgow takes the win, but it doesn't gut me. Ninth in the league. For a team cobbled together a year ago, it's a fucking miracle. I feel the sting of the loss settle in my muscles, more exhaustion than disappointment.

The changing room reeks of sweat and blood and shower gel as I scrub off the full eighty minutes. Thirty-six to Glasgow, our final match of the season. Not a shellacking, but not the fairy tale ending either.

Water sluices down my back as I replay Coach Wallace's post-match speech. 'Not what we deserved, but for a first-year club? We've scared the establishment. Next season, we climb.'

And you bet I'll be here to climb with them.

I shut off the shower and haul my towel off the rail. My muscles ache in that satisfying way that tells me I've given it my all, left everything on the pitch. The boys around me are subdued but not devastated. We know what we're building here.

'Oi, pretty boy,' Connor calls from across the room. 'You coming tonight or has your ball and chain got other plans?'

I flip him the finger as I towel my hair. 'My ball and chain, as you so respectfully call her, has a beautiful name.'

'And the rest of her has your nuts in a vice,' Connor adds, swatting my shoulder as he passes.

'Jealousy's an ugly colour on you.' I pull on my joggers. 'When's the last time a woman waited for you after a match?'

Jamie scoffs in his corner. 'And yer maw doesn't count, Duffy.'

The room erupts in that specific brand of laughter that only exists between men who've bled together often enough. Even Scottie cracks a half-smile, which is rare these days.

'Piss off, the lot of you,' Connor grumbles, but there's no heat in it. 'So, Sin & Tonic at seven? First round's on the captain.'

Brodie groans. 'When did we decide that?'

'Just now,' Scottie pulls on a black tee. 'You can expense it to Charlie.'

'I value my balls too much for that,' Brodie says. 'But I'll inform her of your great idea when she's back from that sponsor meeting, ya prick.'

I laugh and grab my phone. A text from Theo.

> Waiting outside. Brought sustenance. Ready when you are, Sexy MacSwagger. 😘

My heart does that squeeze that it always does when I see her name. Five months together and I'm still like a teenager.

Rucked Up Ruse

'You coming tonight, Finn?' Jamie asks, zipping his kit bag.

'Later, aye. Got something to do first.'

'Something or someone?' Connor waggles his eyebrows.

'Grow up, mate.' But I'm grinning, can't help it. 'We'll be there. Wouldn't wanna miss celebrating the end of the season.'

I grab my bag and head for the exit, ignoring the wolf whistles behind me. The corridor stretches ahead, concrete and fluorescent lights, and then I push through the double doors into the afternoon air.

The whole world sharpens.

Theo leans against the wall, scrolling through her phone. Her dark hair falls in soft waves around her face, and she's wearing a little blue dress dotted with tiny white anchors that hugs every curve. Mary Janes with white socks, like some fantasy librarian come to life.

My cock gives a hopeful twitch. Nope, I'll never get tired of that view. Not even when her hair's white and she walks on a stick.

I'll love this woman for the rest of my life.

She lifts her gaze as the door closes behind me, and her smile hits me square in the chest.

'Hello there, my favourite rugby star.'

I drop my kit bag and pull her against me, breathing in that scent that's become home. 'Hello, List Girl. We lost.'

She reaches into her bag and pulls out a small tin. 'I brought celebratory biscuits.'

I laugh. 'We lost, Theo.'

'These are for finishing your first season without getting arrested or knocked unconscious more than once.' She bops my nose. 'A proper achievement for Finlay Lennox.'

'Fair point.'

Her fingers find my wrist, tracing the small cherry tattoo I got last month.

'I can't believe you did that.'

'It reminds me of you.' I kiss her temple. 'Your blouses. Your lip balm, your soap…'

Five months of learning every inch of her body, of watching her come beneath me, against walls and furniture and countertops. Five months of discovering that sex with one woman – this woman – is more addictive than all the flings that came before combined. Other women have ceased to exist. They're background noise. There's only Theo's frequency, and I'm tuned in all the way.

I pull her closer. 'Sin & Tonic at seven,' I murmur against her ear. 'That gives us a couple hours.'

'Good. Are you ready?' She takes my hand.

'Naw, but let's do it anyway.'

We walk to my car, her heels clicking against the concrete. The BMW chirps as I unlock it. Theo sinks into the seat as if she belongs there. As far as I'm concerned, she does. Preferably straddling me, swearing in that bossy wee voice. I wouldn't have guessed it in a million years, but prim and proper Theodora MacMickin has developed a thing for car sex. And I'm more than happy to oblige.

I toss my kit in the back and settle behind the wheel.

'You know,' she says as I start the engine, 'lesser men would be upset after losing. But you're grinning from ear to ear.'

I reach across and rest my hand on her thigh, feeling goosebumps rise under my palm. 'Other men don't have *you* waiting for them after.'

She rolls her eyes as she always does, but I catch the pleased smile she tries to hide.

I pull out of the car park, my hand still on her leg. The season's over, but something much better is beginning. I never thought I could be this happy with one woman. Never thought I'd stop chasing the next thrill. But Theo MacMickin has me in the palm of her tiny hand.

Rucked Up Ruse

. . .

Fifteen minutes into the drive through Glasgow, I roll down the window and let the air rush in. Theo's singing along to the radio, something indie that she knows all the words to.

'So I've been thinking.' I drum my fingers on the steering wheel as we stop at a red light.

She turns to me, eyebrows raised. 'Is this a threat or a confession? I never know with you.'

'Ha bloody ha. Serious, though. Remember that meeting I had with Charlie last month?'

She tucks a strand of hair behind her ear. 'The one where you both went suspiciously quiet when I came into the room?'

'That's the one. It's about the charity thing, the second part of my redemption arc, as you two called it.' I take a breath. 'I'm starting a foundation.'

Her head snaps toward me. 'A what now?'

'A foundation for children. For weans with parents who have mental health problems.' I keep my eyes on the road but feel her staring at me. 'Kids who need someone to see them, to listen. Who need to know they're not alone.'

I glance over. Theo goes still in the way she does when everything inside her is moving too fast.

'Because of what you told me about your mum. About how you handled her depression all by yourself. How nobody noticed. How you became this tiny adult much too early.'

She blinks once. Then again. Her mouth moves, but she doesn't speak.

'You should've had support, Theo. God knows how many children out there are struggling in silence. I can't go back in time and change your past, but maybe I can change someone's future. It's a surprise.'

When I look again, the tears are already halfway down.

'Ah fuck. Don't cry, baby.' I reach over and brush my thumb across her cheek. 'I'm sorry, I should've asked if—'

'No.' She catches my hand and presses it against her damp face. 'It's perfect.'

I park the car.

'You should include children of parents with addiction,' she adds after a moment. 'Because everything you just said, I'm saying right back at ya.'

'What?'

'Your dad. Your mum. The way you learned to be the loudest person to distract from the pain. How you still sometimes expect everyone to leave.'

She knows me. She knows all of me. I let her know all of me, and it's everything.

'Charlie's already talking to the solicitors,' I say. 'We can set it up however we want. Make it ours.'

'Ours?'

'If you want.' I turn in my seat to face her properly. 'I want you with me on this, Theo.'

She unbuckles her seatbelt and leans across the console. Her lips brush mine. 'I'm with you. Always. Come on, let's go.'

I pull the flowers from the backseat. White carnations. Theo chose them, said they symbolise the restoration of innocence after death. Not so sure about that, but they're better than nothing.

Riddrie Park Cemetery stretches before us, rows of headstones marching across the hillside. The grass is patchy, more brown than green, and the wind bites through my jacket.

Been putting it off long enough.

We follow the path toward the far corner where the common plots sit. My heart pounds. Six months ago, I'd have been gasping for air by now, vision tunnelling, chest constricting. But I'm not alone anymore.

'Row seventeen.' Theo examines the small map she printed. 'Section C.'

No headstones here, just small metal markers with

numbers. The council's efficient solution for those who die with no one to claim them. Or with someone who refuses to.

Like me.

I didn't go searching for his grave. But Theo did. Made calls with the council, filled out forms, tracked down the plot number while I pretended it didn't matter.

'It's this one.' She stops. Nothing to show Grant Lennox ever existed.

The air turns to tar in my throat. 'Bit underwhelming, isn't it?'

Theo stands beside me, patient and present, as I stare at the patch of soil that's covered my father since his funeral almost half a year ago. She knows when to speak and when to let the quiet do its work. But she squeezes my hand, and I'm grateful for it.

'For years, I used to imagine what I'd say to him if I ever got the chance.' The words are scraping my throat. 'Had a whole pissed-off speech prepared about what a fucked-up father he was.'

'And now?'

'Now I'm just tired and sad.' I crouch down. 'I wish I had some clear memories of him, but I don't. Maybe that's for the best.'

'Yeah, maybe.' She crouches beside me.

'After he left, I'd make up stories about where he'd gone. Secret agent. Rock star. Anything but the truth. Addiction and prison.' I touch the earth with my fingertips. 'His father was the same. And his da before him. Men broken by shipyards closing and jobs disappearing. Well, you know.'

'Not an excuse,' Theo says calmly. 'But an explanation. Context matters.'

'Aye.' I place the carnations down. 'He did his best. It wasn't very good, but it is what it is.'

The wind picks up, rustling through the leaves.

'When I was eleven, I tried to visit him in prison. Took

three buses to get there.' The memory still burns. 'He wouldn't see me. The gate staff rang through, and he told them to send me away.'

'Oh, Finn.'

'All my life I thought it was because he didn't care. Now I wonder if he was trying to protect me. From seeing him like that. Or becoming him.'

'Both can be true,' she says. 'People are complicated.'

'Either way, I turned out awright.' I look at Theo, her eyes shining with unshed tears. 'Better than that, actually. I found you.'

We crouch in silence for a moment, before the words I kept inside for so long finally leave me. 'I never got to say I hate you. Or I forgive you. I didn't get to say a damn thing to you. But…it's forgiven,' I say to the patch of earth. 'For my sake and yours.'

In January, I couldn't have imagined speaking those words. Couldn't even have imagined feeling them.

Theo tightens her arms around my waist.

'Bye, Da.' The words are heavy on my tongue. 'I hope you found some peace in the end. Wherever you are now.'

I stand and pull Theo up with me. Her eyes are wet, but she gives me a wobbly smile.

'I'm so proud of you.' She rises on tiptoes to kiss my cheek.

'For what? Rambling at a grave?'

'For breaking the cycle. For being brave enough to feel all this instead of running from it.'

'I do enough running in my professional life, you know.'

She laughs.

I wrap my arms around her, burying my face in her hair. 'You're my family now.'

'And you're mine – and Elvis'.'

I've never belonged to anyone before. But Theo and her fluff demon? I'm theirs for good.

As we walk back to the car, hand in hand, I feel lighter somehow. Not healed – I don't think that's how grief works – but different. As if I've put down something heavy I've been carrying too long.

The cemetery gate creaks as we pass through. I glance at Theo, this woman who tracked down my father's grave, who holds me through nightmares, who loves me not despite my damage but somehow because of it.

Later, we'll join the Stirling Rebels at the Sin & Tonic to celebrate the season. I'll watch Theo disarm Connor with her quick wit and make Brodie smile. Perhaps she's in the mood to eviscerate someone at the pool table.

Aye, I like it when she does that.

But right now, this moment is enough. Her hand in mine, the promise of tomorrow.

I spent my whole life trying to outrun pain, outdrink memory, outfuck loneliness. Theo didn't save me, she just held me. She walked into my life with her lists and her laughter and her impossible belief in me. Even when I didn't deserve it.

Love is not the absence of pain. It's choosing someone worth hurting for, worth staying for, working through it together.

I'd walk through hell to keep her safe. To make her proud. To be the man she sees when she looks at me. Loving Theo is the only thing that's ever made me feel like I'm more than the damage I carry. And that's not running. That's coming home.

— THE END —

∽

Don't miss out on part 1 of the series – Brodie and Charlie's story. **Read *Tackled by Trouble!***

Beatrice Bradshaw

🔔 Get notified when book 3 drops and sign up here – beatricebradshaw.com/rucked-up

Interested in more spicy and cosy Scottish romance? Check out my 'Escape to Scotland' series of standalone books:

Book 1: *Love in the Scottish Winter Highlands*
Book 2: *Love on the Scottish Spring Isle*
Book 3: *Love on the Scottish Summer Coast*
Book 4: *Love in the Scottish Fall Forest*
Book 5: *Love in the Scottish Christmas Village*

Thank you so much for reading. If you liked Finn and Theo's story, please take a minute to leave a review on Amazon or Goodreads. Love! <3

Glossary

- aboot = about
- anyhoo = anyhow
- Auld Reekie = Edinburgh ('Old Smoky')
- awfy = very; can mean 'awful' but more often used as an intensifier
- awright = all right
- bampot = a fool, a mad person
- baws = balls, aka testicles
- belter = something fantastic and extremely good
- boaby = penis
- braw = great, beautiful
- calm doon = calm down
- ceilidh = Scottish country dance in groups and pairs
- cranachan = traditional Scottish dessert with raspberries
- da = dad
- daft = silly, foolish, stupid
- deid = dead
- dinnae/ disnae = don't/ doesn't
- eejit = idiot
- fae = from

Glossary

- faffin' aboot = to spend time doing things that are not important
- fanny = foolish person, vagina, pejorative – also used as a form of endearment
- gobshite = blabbering fool
- gonnae = going to
- greetin' = crying, whining
- hame = home
- heid = head
- Hogmanay = New Year's Eve
- ken = know
- maw = mum
- mews = a house that originated as stable or carriage house behind a larger residence
- minging = gross, disgusting
- naw/ nae = no
- numpty = foolish person
- Ochils = range of hills north of the Forth valley
- pished = drunk
- polis = police
- schemes = council housing, like the projects in the US
- steamin' = very drunk
- tadger = slang word for a penis
- taking a beamer = blushing
- walloper = derogatory term for a penis, used to describe someone as a fool or nuisance
- wee chancer = someone who gets away with things
- Wreck the Hoose Juice = Buckfast; caffeinated alcoholic drink made of fortified wine with added caffeine

Resource:
  Dictionary of the Scottish Language https://dsl.ac.uk/

Author's note

Dearest reader,

Thank you so much for picking up *Rucked Up Ruse*. I hope you enjoyed Finn and Theo's moving story.

If you're not sure what a ruck is, picture a group of rugby players in a heap, boots everywhere, bodies straining, all trying to get their hands on the ball without breaking too many bones. That's the official definition. The unofficial one is: glorious chaos. And so it made the perfect title for a fake dating romance between a control freak with a core of butter and a wild player with a heart of gold.

As you might or might not know, Theo was never meant to be in the middle of this chaos or this series. In *Tackled by Trouble*, she was just supposed to open the door for Brodie, say hello, and disappear. Finn was supposed to make eyes at Ailsa.

But Theo had other ideas. She made friends with Charlie, settled in, and started giving Finn these sideways glances in my head. And he was looking right back. At some point, I stopped arguing and just let them get on with it. It became obvious the next story had to be theirs.

Author's note

Even though all the character's are entirely fictional, Finn is loosely inspired by the kind of athlete Dennis Rodman embodied in the 1990s Chicago Bulls era: wild, volatile, emotionally raw, a little rebellious, irreplaceable, devastatingly charming, and all heart under the chaos. A man who's a complete headache for PR but magnetic enough to get away with it.

At the end of *Tackled by Trouble*, I knew Finn had gone AWOL. But I didn't know where or why. He later told me in the shower (as characters tend to do, uninvited). His dad had just died in Barlinnie, the largest prison in Scotland. Maybe that came to my subconscious because I'd just had my *fourth* jury citation since moving to Scotland. Who knows?

So yeah, addiction and imprisonment are part of this book. It's not all kilts, stags, and cosy ceilidhs in Scotland. There's a bit of *Trainspotting*, too.

Much can be debated about the roots of deprivation and addiction. Genetics, yes, social circumstances, but as a historian, I can't help pointing out that large-scale industrialisation from the 1800s and then deindustrialisation in the '60s and '70s left deep marks on Scottish communities. Scotland's journey from industrial powerhouse to post-industrial decline, and now two decades into a new millennium, has left its mark. You see it in places and in people – like Finn.

As always with my books, some of my own story found its way in too. Members of my family have been living with addiction and depression for most of their lives. When I was fifteen, I moved in with my grandparents. So I know a little of both Theo and Finn's pain.

I think we all carry our pasts with us. We're like trees that have grown around fences and stones. Twisted into shapes we didn't choose, but stronger, and sometimes more beautiful and unique, because of it.

Also, if you've ever had a cat, you'll know exactly what's going on in the kitchen scene.

Author's note

So, I hope you fall for Finn and Theo the way I did, unexpectedly and completely.

With love – and a healthy respect for a proper ruck,

Beatrice

About the Author

Beatrice Bradshaw crafts spicy contemporary romances set across Scotland – whisking readers away to glens and windswept coastlines without the need for a plane ticket!

Photo: Kristy Ashton

By day, she's a German journalist, translator, and Scottish historian; by night, she transforms into a purveyor of page-turning passion and fun.

Beatrice Bradshaw is the pen name/ pseudonym of Jessica Beatrice Wagener – chosen so as not to have German narrative non-fiction confused with her (English) romance books.

And after trading Berlin for Scotland in 2018, Beatrice has been smitten with her adopted homeland and not once looked back.

With her knowledge of Scottish history and literature acquired at the University of Glasgow, she sprinkles authentic Scottish experiences through stories that venture well beyond predictable clichés. Her heroines are fierce, funny, and delightfully flawed. The kind of women who trip over their own witty comebacks but land on their feet with style. Her books deliver wit, heat, and men who are actually worth the emotional investment: charming, filthy, and capable of both finding the G-spot and the grocery store without assistance.

When not hunched over her laptop in her Glasgow flat (fuelled by industrial amounts of coffee and pastries), you'll find her hunting for inspiration in crumbling castles, exploring Scottish landscapes, or striking up conversations with the residents of ancient cemeteries. Her future gravestone will immortalise the time she convinced David Hasselhoff to sing, a tale best shared over whisky. And while she throws herself into ceilidhs with the same enthusiasm as karaoke nights, her dancing has been described as 'enthusiastically hazardous'.

Connect with Beatrice here:
instagram.com/beatricebradshawauthor
facebook.com/beatricebradshawauthor
www.beatricebradshaw.com

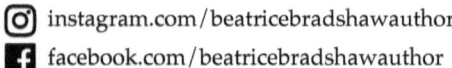

instagram.com/beatricebradshawauthor
facebook.com/beatricebradshawauthor

Rucked Up Ruse
By Beatrice Bradshaw

First published in the UK by Jessica B. Wagener under the pen name Beatrice Bradshaw 2025. Copyright © Jessica B. Wagener as Beatrice Bradshaw, 2025

Suite 624
Claymore House
145-149 Kilmarnock Road
Glasgow, G41 3JA

Jessica B. Wagener as Beatrice Bradshaw has asserted her right to be identified as the author of this work.

All rights reserved. No part of this publication may be reproduced, transmitted, or stored in any retrieval system, in any form or by any means, electronic, mechanical, photocopying, recording or otherwise, without the prior written permission of the publisher/ author, except for the use of brief quotations in a book review.

This book is a work of fiction. Names, characters, businesses, organisations, places, incidents, and events other than those clearly in the public domain, are either the product of the author's imagination or are used fictitiously and are not to be construed as real. Any resemblance to actual persons, living or dead, events or locales is coincidental.

Proof reading: Micki McNie

Cover design: Jessica Wagener

Illustration: Richard Jackson

Print ISBN: 978-1-9191845-0-0
Ebook Edition © August 2025
ISBN: 978-1-0685768-9-8
Version: 2025-08-19

www.ingramcontent.com/pod-product-compliance
Lightning Source LLC
Chambersburg PA
CBHW020401080526
44584CB00014B/1124